SELECTED WORKS

SIGNATURE EDITIONS

SELECTED WORKS

LUCIUS ANNAEUS SENECA

UNION
SQUARE
& CO.

NEW YORK

UNION
SQUARE
& CO.

NEW YORK

UNION SQUARE & CO. and the distinctive Union Square & Co. logo
are trademarks of Sterling Publishing Co., Inc.

Union Square & Co., LLC, is a subsidiary of Sterling Publishing Co., Inc.

This 2024 edition published by Union Square & Co.

ISBN 978-1-4351-7300-2

For information about custom editions, special sales, and premium
purchases, please contact specialsales@unionsquareandco.com.

Printed in India

2 4 6 8 10 9 7 5 3

unionsquareandco.com

Cover design by Igor Satanovsky and David Ter-Avanesyan
Cover images: Prismatic Pictures/Bridgeman Images,
Fresh Take Design/Shutterstock.com

CONTENTS

MINOR DIALOGUES OF SENECA
translated by Aubrey Stewart, M.A.

SELECTED LETTERS FROM A STOIC
translated by Richard M. Grummere, Ph.D.

CONTENTS

MINOR DIALOGUES
OF SENECA

Translated by Aubrey Stewart, M.A.

OF PROVIDENCE

ADDRESSED TO LUCILIUS

1.   You have asked me, Lucilius, why, if the world be ruled by
     providence, so many evils befall good men? The answer to
     this would be more conveniently given in the course of this
     work, after we have proved that providence governs the uni-
     verse, and that God is amongst us: but, since you wish me
     to deal with one point apart from the whole, and to answer
     one replication before the main action has been decided, I
     will do what is not difficult, and plead the cause of the gods.
     At the present time it is superfluous to point out that it is
     not without some guardian that so great a work maintains its
     position, that the assemblage and movements of the stars do
     not depend upon accidental impulses, or that objects whose
     motion is regulated by chance often fall into confusion and
     soon stumble, whereas this swift and safe movement goes
     on, governed by eternal law, bearing with it so many things
     both on sea and land, so many most brilliant lights shining in
     order in the skies; that this regularity does not belong to mat-
     ter moving at random, and that particles brought together
     by chance could not arrange themselves with such art as to
     make the heaviest weight, that of the earth, remain unmoved,
     and behold the flight of the heavens as they hasten round
     it, to make the seas pour into the valleys and so temper the
     climate of the land, without any sensible increase from the

rivers which flow into them, or to cause huge growths to proceed from minute seeds. Even those phenomena which appear to be confused and irregular, I mean showers of rain and clouds, the rush of lightning from the heavens, fire that pours from the riven peaks of mountains, quakings of the trembling earth, and everything else which is produced on earth by the unquiet element in the universe, do not come to pass without reason, though they do so suddenly: but they also have their causes, as also have those things which excite our wonder by the strangeness of their position, such as warm springs amidst the waves of the sea, and new islands that spring up in the wide ocean. Moreover, any one who has watched how the shore is laid bare by the retreat of the sea into itself, and how within a short time it is again covered, will believe that it is in obedience to some hidden law of change that the waves are at one time contracted and driven inwards, at another burst forth and regain their bed with a strong current, since all the while they wax in regular proportion, and come up at their appointed day and hour greater or less, according as the moon, at whose pleasure the ocean flows, draws them. Let these matters be set aside for discussion at their own proper season, but I, since you do not doubt the existence of providence but complain of it, will on that account more readily reconcile you to gods who are most excellent to excellent men: for indeed the nature of things does not ever permit good to be injured by good. Between good men and the gods there is a friendship which is brought about by virtue—friendship do I say? nay, rather relationship and likeness, since the good man differs from a god in time alone, being his pupil and rival and true offspring, whom his glorious parent trains more severely than other men, insisting sternly on virtuous conduct, just as strict fathers do. When therefore you see men who are good and acceptable to the gods toiling, sweating, painfully struggling upwards, while bad men run riot and are steeped in pleasures, reflect that modesty pleases us in our sons, and forwardness in our house-born slave-boys; that the former are held in check by a somewhat stern rule, whereas the boldness of the latter is encouraged. Be thou sure that God acts in like manner: He does not pet the good man: He tries him, hardens him, and fits him for Himself.

2. Why do many things turn out badly for good men? Why, no evil can befall a good man: contraries cannot combine. Just as so many rivers, so many showers of rain from the clouds, such a number of medicinal springs, do not alter the taste of the sea, indeed, do not so much as soften it, so the pressure of adversity does not affect the mind of a brave man; for the mind of a brave man maintains its balance and throws its own complexion over all that takes place, because it is more powerful than any external circumstances. I do not say that he does not feel them, but he conquers them, and on occasion calmly and tranquilly rises superior to their attacks, holding all misfortunes to be trials of his own firmness. Yet who is there who, provided he be a man and have honourable ambition, does not long for due employment, and is not eager to do his duty in spite of danger? Is there any hardworking man to whom idleness is not a punishment? We see athletes, who study only their bodily strength, engage in contests with the strongest of men, and insist that those who train them for the arena should put out their whole strength when practising with them: they endure blows and maltreatment, and, if they cannot find any single person who is their match, they engage with several at once: their strength and courage droop without an antagonist: they can only prove how great and how mighty it is by proving how much they can endure. You should know that good men ought to act in like manner, so as not to fear troubles and difficulties, nor to lament their hard fate, to take in good part whatever befalls them, and force it to become a blessing to them. It does not matter what you bear, but how you bear it. Do you not see how differently fathers and mothers indulge their children?

how the former urge them to begin their tasks betimes, will not suffer them to be idle even on holidays, and exercise them till they perspire, and sometimes till they shed tears—while their mothers want to cuddle them in their laps, and keep them out of the sun, and never wish them to be vexed, or to cry, or to work. God bears a fatherly mind towards good men, and loves them in a manly spirit. "Let them," says He, "be exercised by labours, sufferings, and losses, that so they may gather true strength." Those who are surfeited with ease break down not only with labour, but with mere motion and by their own weight. Unbroken prosperity cannot bear a single blow; but he who has waged an unceasing strife with his misfortunes has gained a thicker skin by his sufferings, yields to no disaster, and even though he fall yet fights on his knee. Do you wonder that God, who so loves the good, who would have them attain the highest goodness and pre-eminence, should appoint fortune to be their adversary? I should not be surprised if the gods sometimes experience a wish to behold great men struggling with some misfortune. We sometimes are delighted when a youth of steady courage receives on his spear the wild beast that attacks him; or when he meets the charge of a lion without flinching; and the more eminent the man is who acts thus, the more attractive is the sight: yet these are not matters which can attract the attention of the gods, but are mere pastime and diversions of human frivolity. Behold a sight worthy to be viewed by a god interested in his own work, behold a pair worthy of a god, a brave man matched with evil fortune, especially if he himself has given the challenge. I say, I do not know what nobler spectacle Jupiter could find on earth, should he turn his eyes thither, than that of Cato, after his party had more than once been defeated, still standing upright amid the ruins of the commonwealth. Quoth he, "What though all be fallen into one man's power, though the land be guarded by his legions, the sea by his fleets, though Caesar's soldiers beset the city gate? Cato has a way out of it: with one hand he will open a wide path to freedom; his sword, which he has borne unstained by disgrace and innocent of crime even in a civil war, will still perform good and noble deeds; it will give to Cato that freedom which it could not give to his country. Begin, my soul, the work which thou so long hast contemplated, snatch thyself away from the world of man. Already Petreius and Juba have met and fallen, each slain by the other's hand—a brave and noble compact with fate, yet not one befitting my greatness: it is as disgraceful for Cato to beg his death of any one as it would be for him to beg his life."

It is clear to me that the gods must have looked on with great joy, while that man, his own most ruthless avenger, took thought for the safety of others and arranged the escape of those who departed, while even on his last night he pursued his studies, while he drove the sword into his sacred breast, while he tore forth his vitals and laid his hand upon that most holy life which was unworthy to be defiled by steel. This, I am inclined to think, was the reason that his wound was not well-aimed and mortal: the gods were not satisfied with seeing Cato die once: his courage was kept in action and recalled to the stage, that it might display itself in a more difficult part: for it needs a greater mind to return a second time to death. How could they fail to view their pupil with interest when leaving his life by such a noble and memorable departure? Men are raised to the level of the gods by a death which is admired even by those who fear them.

3. However, as my argument proceeds, I shall prove that what appear to be evils are not so; for the present I say this, that what you call hard measure, misfortunes, and things against which we ought to pray, are really to the advantage, firstly, of those to whom they happen, and secondly, of all mankind, for whom the gods care more than for individuals; and next, that these evils befall them with their own good will, and that men deserve to endure misfortunes, if they are unwilling to receive them. To this I shall add, that misfortunes proceed

thus by destiny, and that they befall good men by the same law which makes them good. After this, I shall prevail upon you never to pity any good man; for though he may be called unhappy, he cannot be so.

Of all these propositions that which I have stated first appears the most difficult to prove, I mean, that the things which we dread and shudder at are to the advantage of those to whom they happen. "Is it," say you, "to their advantage to be driven into exile, to be brought to want, to carry out to burial their children and wife, to be publicly disgraced, to lose their health?" Yes! if you are surprised at these being to any man's advantage, you will also be surprised at any man being benefited by the knife and cautery, or by hunger and thirst as well. Yet if you consider that some men, in order to be cured, have their bones scraped, and pieces of them extracted, that their veins are pulled out, and that some have limbs cut off, which could not remain in their place without ruin to the whole body, you will allow me to prove to you this also, that some misfortunes are for the good of those to whom they happen, just as much, by Hercules, as some things which are praised and sought after are harmful to those who enjoy them, like indigestions and drunkenness and other matters which kill us through pleasure. Among many grand sayings of our Demetrius is this, which I have but just heard, and which still rings and thrills in my ears: "No one," said he, "seems to me more unhappy than the man whom no misfortune has ever befallen." He never has had an opportunity of testing himself; though everything has happened to him according to his wish, nay, even before he has formed a wish, yet the gods have judged him unfavourably; he has never been deemed worthy to conquer ill fortune, which avoids the greatest cowards, as though it said, "Why should I take that man for my antagonist? He will straightaway lay down his arms: I shall not need all my strength against him: he will be put to flight by a mere menace: he dares not even face me; let me look around for some other with whom I may fight hand to hand: I blush to join battle with one who is prepared to be beaten." A gladiator deems it a disgrace to be matched with an inferior, and knows that to win without danger is to win without glory. Just so doth Fortune; she seeks out the bravest to match herself with, passes over some with disdain, and makes for the most unyielding and upright of men, to exert her strength against them. She tried Mucius by fire, Fabricius by poverty, Rutilius by exile, Regulus by torture, Socrates by poison, Cato by death: it is ill fortune alone that discovers these glorious examples. Was Mucius unhappy, because he grasped the enemy's fire with his right hand, and of his own accord paid the penalty of his mistake? because he overcame the King with his hand when it was burned, though he could not when it held a sword? Would he have been happier, if he had warmed his hand in his mistress's bosom? Was Fabricius unhappy, because when the state could spare him, he dug his own land? because he waged war against riches as keenly as against Pyrrhus? because he supped beside his hearth off the very roots and herbs which he himself, though an old man, and one who had enjoyed a triumph, had grubbed up while clearing his field of weeds? What then? would he have been happier if he had gorged himself with fishes from distant shores, and birds caught in foreign lands? if he had roused the torpor of his queasy stomach with shellfish from the upper and the lower sea? if he had piled a great heap of fruits round game of the first head, which many huntsmen had been killed in capturing? Was Rutilius unhappy, because those who condemned him will have to plead their cause for all ages? because he endured the loss of his country more composedly than that of his banishment? because he was the only man who refused anything to Sulla the dictator, and when recalled from exile all but went further away and banished himself still more. "Let those," said he, "whom thy fortunate reign catches at Rome, see to the Forum drenched with blood, and the heads of Senators above the Pool of Servilius—the place where the victims of Sulla's proscriptions were stripped—the bands of assassins roaming at large through the city, and many thousands of Roman citizens slaughtered in one place, after, nay, by means of a promise of quarter. Let those who are unable to go into exile behold these things." Well! is Lucius Sulla happy, because when he comes down into the Forum room is made for him with sword-strokes, because he allows the heads of consulars to be shown to him, and counts out the price of blood through the quaestor and the state exchequer? And this, this was the man who passed the Lex Cornelia! Let us now come to Regulus: what injury did fortune do him when she made him an example of good faith, an example of endurance? They pierce his skin with nails: wherever he leans his weary body, it rests on a wound; his eyes are fixed forever open; the greater his sufferings, the greater is his glory. Would you know how far he is from regretting that he valued his honour at such a price? heal his wounds and send him again into the senate house; he will give the same advice. So, then, you think Maecenas a happier man, who when troubled by love, and weeping at the daily repulses of his ill-natured wife, sought for sleep by listening to distant strains of music? Though he drug himself with wine, divert himself with the sound of falling waters, and distract his troubled thoughts with a thousand pleasures, yet Maecenas will no more sleep on his down cushions than Regulus on the rack. Yet it consoles the latter that he suffers for the sake of honour, and he looks away from his torments to their cause: whilst the other, jaded with pleasures and sick with over-enjoyment, is more hurt by the cause of his sufferings than by the sufferings themselves. Vice has not so utterly taken possession of the human race that, if men were allowed to choose their destiny, there can be any doubt but that more would choose to be Reguluses than to be Maecenases: or if there were any one who dared to say that he would prefer to be born Maecenas than Regulus, that man, whether he says so or not, would rather have been Terentia (than Cicero).

Do you consider Socrates to have been badly used, because he took that draught which the state assigned to him as though it were a charm to make him immortal, and argued about death until death itself? Was he ill treated, because his blood froze and the current of his veins gradually stopped as the chill of death crept over them? How much more is this man to be envied than he who is served on precious stones, whose drink a creature trained to every vice, a eunuch or much the same, cools with snow in a golden cup? Such men as these bring up again all that they drink, in misery and disgust at the taste of their own bile, while Socrates cheerfully and willingly drains his poison. As for Cato, enough has been said, and all men must agree that the highest happiness was reached by one who was chosen by Nature herself as worthy to contend with all her terrors: "The enmity," says she, "of the powerful is grievous, therefore let him be opposed at once by Pompeius, Caesar, and Crassus: it is grievous, when a candidate for public offices, to be defeated by one's inferiors; therefore let him be defeated by Vatinius: it is grievous to take part in civil wars, therefore let him fight in every part of the world for the good cause with equal obstinacy and ill luck: it is grievous to lay hands upon one's self, therefore let him do so. What shall I gain by this? That all men may know that these things, which I have deemed Cato worthy to undergo, are not real evils."

4. Prosperity comes to the mob, and to low-minded men as well as to great ones; but it is the privilege of great men alone to send under the yoke the disasters and terrors of mortal life: whereas to be always prosperous, and to pass through life without a twinge of mental distress, is to remain ignorant of one half of nature. You are a great man; but how am I to know it, if fortune gives you no opportunity of showing your virtue? You have entered the arena of the Olympic games, but no one else has done so: you have the crown, but not the victory: I do not congratulate you as I would a brave man, but

as one who has obtained a consulship or praetorship. You have gained dignity. I may say the same of a good man, if troublesome circumstances have never given him a single opportunity of displaying the strength of his mind. I think you unhappy because you never have been unhappy: you have passed through your life without meeting an antagonist: no one will know your powers, not even you yourself." For a man cannot know himself without a trial: no one ever learned what he could do without putting himself to the test; for which reason many have of their own free will exposed themselves to misfortunes which no longer came in their way, and have sought for an opportunity of making their virtue, which otherwise would have been lost in darkness, shine before the world. Great men, I say, often rejoice at crosses of fortune just as brave soldiers do at wars. I remember to have heard Triumphus, who was a gladiator in the reign of Tiberius Caesar, complaining about the scarcity of prizes; "What a glorious time," said he, "is past." Valour is greedy of danger, and thinks only of whither it strives to go, not of what it will suffer, since even what it will suffer is part of its glory. Soldiers pride themselves on their wounds, they joyously display their blood flowing over their breastplate. Though those who return unwounded from battle may have done as bravely, yet he who returns wounded is more admired. God, I say, favours those whom He wishes to enjoy the greatest honours, whenever He affords them the means of performing some exploit with spirit and courage, something which is not easily to be accomplished: you can judge of a pilot in a storm, of a soldier in a battle. How can I know with how great a spirit you could endure poverty, if you overflow with riches? How can I tell with how great firmness you could bear up against disgrace, dishonour, and public hatred, if you grow old to the sound of applause, if popular favour cannot be alienated from you, and seems to flow to you by the natural bent of men's minds? How can I know how calmly you would endure to be childless, if you see all your children around you? I have heard what you said when you were consoling others: then I should have seen whether you could have consoled yourself, whether you could have forbidden yourself to grieve. Do not, I beg you, dread those things which the immortal gods apply to our minds like spurs: misfortune is virtue's opportunity. Those men may justly be called unhappy who are stupefied with excess of enjoyment, whom sluggish contentment keeps as it were becalmed in a quiet sea: whatever befalls them will come strange to them. Misfortunes press hardest on those who are unacquainted with them: the yoke feels heavy to the tender neck. The recruit turns pale at the thought of a wound: the veteran, who knows that he has often won the victory after losing blood, looks boldly at his own flowing gore. In like manner God hardens, reviews, and exercises those whom He tests and loves: those whom He seems to indulge and spare, He is keeping out of condition to meet their coming misfortunes: for you are mistaken if you suppose that anyone is exempt from misfortune: he who has long prospered will have his share some day; those who seem to have been spared them have only had them put off. Why does God afflict the best of men with ill health, or sorrow, or other troubles? Because in the army the most hazardous services are assigned to the bravest soldiers: a general sends his choicest troops to attack the enemy in a midnight ambuscade, to reconnoitre his line of march, or to drive the hostile garrisons from their strong places. No one of these men says as he begins his march, "The general has dealt hardly with me," but "He has judged well of me." Let those who are bidden to suffer what makes the weak and cowardly weep, say likewise, "God has thought us worthy subjects on whom to try how much suffering human nature can endure." Avoid luxury, avoid effeminate enjoyment, by which men's minds are softened, and in which, unless something occurs to remind them of the common lot of humanity, they lie unconscious, as though plunged in continual drunkenness. He whom glazed windows have always guarded from the wind, whose feet are warmed by constantly renewed fomentations, whose dining room is heated by hot air beneath the floor and spread through the walls, cannot meet the gentlest breeze without danger. While all excesses are hurtful, excess of comfort is the most hurtful of all; it affects the brain; it leads men's minds into vain imaginings; it spreads a thick cloud over the boundaries of truth and falsehood. Is it not better, with virtue by one's side, to endure continual misfortune, than to burst with an endless surfeit of good things? It is the overloaded stomach that is rent asunder: death treats starvation more gently. The gods deal with good men according to the same rule as schoolmasters with their pupils, who exact most labour from those of whom they have the surest hopes. Do you imagine that the Lacedaemonians, who test the mettle of their children by public flogging, do not love them? Their own fathers call upon them to endure the strokes of the rod bravely, and when they are torn and half dead, ask them to offer their wounded skin to receive fresh wounds. Why then should we wonder if God tries noble spirits severely? There can be no easy proof of virtue. Fortune lashes and mangles us: well, let us endure it: it is not cruelty, it is a struggle, in which the oftener we engage the braver we shall become. The strongest part of the body is that which is exercised by the most frequent use: we must entrust ourselves to fortune to be hardened by her against herself: by degrees she will make us a match for herself. Familiarity with danger leads us to despise it. Thus the bodies of sailors are hardened by endurance of the sea, and the hands of farmers by work; the arms of soldiers are powerful to hurl darts, the legs of runners are active: that part of each man which he exercises is the strongest: so by endurance the mind becomes able to despise the power of misfortunes. You may see what endurance might effect in us if you observe what labour does among tribes that are naked and rendered stronger by want. Look at all the nations that dwell beyond the Roman Empire: I mean the Germans and all the nomad tribes that war against us along the Danube. They suffer from eternal winter, and a dismal climate, the barren soil grudges them sustenance, they keep off the rain with leaves or thatch, they bound across frozen marshes, and hunt wild beasts for food. Do you think them unhappy? There is no unhappiness in what use has made part of one's nature: by degrees men find pleasure in doing what they were first driven to do by necessity. They have no homes and no resting places save those which weariness appoints them for the day; their food, though coarse, yet must be sought with their own hands; the harshness of the climate is terrible, and their bodies are unclothed. This, which you think a hardship, is the mode of life of all these races: how then can you wonder at good men being shaken, in order that they may be strengthened? No tree which the wind does not often blow against is firm and strong; for it is stiffened by the very act of being shaken, and plants its roots more securely: those which grow in a sheltered valley are brittle: and so it is to the advantage of good men, and causes them to be undismayed, that they should live much amidst alarms, and learn to bear with patience what is not evil save to him who endures it ill.

5. Add to this that it is to the advantage of everyone that the best men should, so to speak, be on active service and perform labours: God has the same purpose as the wise man, that is, to prove that the things which the herd covets and dreads are neither good nor bad in themselves. If, however, He only bestows them upon good men, it will be evident that they are good things, and bad, if He only inflicts them upon bad men. Blindness would be execrable if no one lost his eyes except those who deserve to have them pulled out; therefore let Appius and Metellus be doomed to darkness. Riches are not a good thing: therefore let Elius the pander possess them, that men who have consecrated money in the temple, may see the same in the brothel: for by no means can God discredit objects of desire so effectually as by bestowing

them upon the worst of men, and removing them from the best. "But," you say, "it is unjust that a good man should be enfeebled, or transfixed, or chained, while bad men swagger at large with a whole skin." What! is it not unjust that brave men should bear arms, pass the night in camps, and stand on guard along the rampart with their wounds still bandaged, while within the city eunuchs and professional profligates live at their ease? what? is it not unjust that maidens of the highest birth should be roused at night to perform Divine service, while fallen women enjoy the soundest sleep? Labour calls for the best man: the senate often passes the whole day in debate, while at the same time every scoundrel either amuses his leisure in the Campus Martius, or lurks in a tavern, or passes his time in some pleasant society. The same thing happens in this great commonwealth (of the world): good men labour, spend and are spent, and that too of their own free will; they are not dragged along by fortune, but follow her and take equal steps with her; if they knew how, they would outstrip her. I remember, also, to have heard this spirited saying of that stoutest-hearted of men, Demetrius. "Ye immortal Gods," said he, "the only complaint which I have to make of you is that you did not make your will known to me earlier; for then I would sooner have gone into that state of life to which I now have been called. Do you wish to take my children? it was for you that I brought them up. Do you wish to take some part of my body? take it: it is no great thing that I am offering you, I shall soon have done with the whole of it. Do you wish for my life? why should I hesitate to return to you what you gave me? whatever you ask you shall receive with my good will: nay, I would rather give it than be forced to hand it over to you: what need had you to take away what you did? you might have received it from me: yet even as it is you cannot take anything from me, because you cannot rob a man unless he resists."

I am constrained to nothing, I suffer nothing against my will, nor am I God's slave, but his willing follower, and so much the more because I know that everything is ordained and proceeds according to a law that endures forever. The fates guide us, and the length of every man's days is decided at the first hour of his birth: every cause depends upon some earlier cause: one long chain of destiny decides all things, public or private. Wherefore, everything must be patiently endured, because events do not fall in our way, as we imagine, but come by a regular law. It has long ago been settled at what you should rejoice and at what you should weep, and although the lives of individual men appear to differ from one another in a great variety of particulars, yet the sum total comes to one and the same thing: we soon perish, and the gifts which we receive soon perish. Why, then, should we be angry? why should we lament? we are prepared for our fate: let nature deal as she will with her own bodies; let us be cheerful whatever befalls, and stoutly reflect that it is not anything of our own that perishes. What is the duty of a good man? to submit himself to fate: it is a great consolation to be swept away together with the entire universe: whatever law is laid upon us that thus we must live and thus we must die, is laid upon the gods also: one unchangeable stream bears along men and gods alike: the creator and ruler of the universe himself, though he has given laws to the fates, yet is guided by them: he always obeys, he only once commanded. "But why was God so unjust in His distribution of fate, as to assign poverty, wounds, and untimely deaths to good men?" The workman cannot alter his materials: this is their nature. Some qualities cannot be separated from some others: they cling together; are indivisible. Dull minds, tending to sleep or to a waking state exactly like sleep, are composed of sluggish elements: it requires stronger stuff to form a man meriting careful description. His course will not be straightforward; he must go upwards and downwards, be tossed about, and guide his vessel through troubled waters: he must make his way in spite of fortune: he will meet with much that is hard which he must soften, much that is rough that he must make smooth. Fire tries gold, misfortune tries brave men. See how high virtue has to climb: you may be sure that it has no safe path to tread.

> Steep is the path at first: the steeds, though strong,
> Fresh from their rest, can hardly crawl along;
> The middle part lies through the topmost sky,
> Whence oft, as I the earth and sea descry,
> I shudder, terrors through my bosom thrill.
> The ending of the path is sheer down hill,
> And needs the careful guidance of the rein,
> Forever when I sink beneath the main,
> Old Tethys trembles in her depths below
> Lest headlong down upon her I should go.

When the spirited youth heard this, he said, "I have no fault to find with the road: I will mount it, it is worthwhile to go through these places, even though one fall." His father did not cease from trying to scare his brave spirit with terrors:—

> Then, too, that thou may'st hold thy course aright,
> And neither turn aside to left nor right,
> Straight through the Bull's fell horns thy path must go,
> Through the fierce Lion, and the Archer's bow.

After this Phaethon says:—

> Harness the chariot which you yield to me,

I am encouraged by these things with which you think to scare me: I long to stand where the Sun himself trembles to stand." It is the part of grovellers and cowards to follow the safe track; courage loves a lofty path.

6. "Yet, why does God permit evil to happen to good men?" He does not permit it: he takes away from them all evils, such as

crimes and scandalous wickedness, daring thoughts, grasp-
ing schemes, blind lusts, and avarice coveting its neighbour's
goods. He protects and saves them. Does anyone besides this
demand that God should look after the baggage of good men
also? Why, they themselves leave the care of this to God: they
scorn external accessories. Democritus forswore riches, holding them to be a burden to a virtuous mind: what wonder
then, if God permits that to happen to a good man, which
a good man sometimes chooses should happen to himself?
Good men, you say, lose their children: why should they not,
since sometimes they even put them to death? They are banished: why should they not be, since sometimes they leave
their country of their own free will, never to return? They
are slain: why not, since sometimes they choose to lay violent
hands on themselves? Why do they suffer certain miseries?
it is that they may teach others how to do so. They are born
as patterns. Conceive, therefore, that God says:—"You, who
have chosen righteousness, what complaint can you make of
me? I have encompassed other men with unreal good things,
and have deceived their inane minds as it were by a long and
misleading dream: I have bedecked them with gold, silver,
and ivory, but within them there is no good thing. Those men
whom you regard as fortunate, if you could see, not their outward show, but their hidden life, are really unhappy, mean,
and base, ornamented on the outside like the walls of their
houses: that good fortune of theirs is not sound and genuine:
it is only a veneer, and that a thin one. As long, therefore,
as they can stand upright and display themselves as they
choose, they shine and impose upon one; when something
occurs to shake and unmask them, we see how deep and real
a rottenness was hidden by that factitious magnificence. To
you I have given sure and lasting good things, which become
greater and better the more one turns them over and views
them on every side: I have granted to you to scorn danger,
to disdain passion. You do not shine outwardly, all your
good qualities are turned inwards; even so does the world

neglect what lies without it, and rejoices in the contemplation of itself. I have placed every good thing within your own
breasts: it is your good fortune not to need any good fortune.
'Yet many things befall you which are sad, dreadful, hard to
be borne.' Well, as I have not been able to remove these from
your path, I have given your minds strength to combat all:
bear them bravely. In this you can surpass God himself; He
is beyond suffering evil: you are above it. Despise poverty;
no man lives as poor as he was born: despise pain; either it
will cease or you will cease: despise death; it either ends you
or takes you elsewhere: despise fortune; I have given her no
weapon that can reach the mind. Above all, I have taken care
that no one should hold you captive against your will: the
way of escape lies open before you: if you do not choose to
fight, you may fly. For this reason, of all those matters which
I have deemed essential for you, I have made nothing easier
for you than to die. I have set man's life as it were on a mountain side: it soon slips down. Do but watch, and you will see
how short and how ready a path leads to freedom. I have not
imposed such long delays upon those who quit the world as
upon those who enter it: were it not so, fortune would hold
a wide dominion over you, if a man died as slowly as he is
born. Let all time, let every place teach you, how simple it is
to renounce nature, and to fling back her gifts to her: before
the altar itself and during the solemn rites of sacrifice, while
life is being prayed for, learn how to die. Fat oxen fall dead
with a tiny wound; a blow from a man's hand fells animals of
great strength: the sutures of the neck are severed by a thin
blade, and when the joint which connects the head and neck
is cut, all that great mass falls. The breath of life is not deep-
seated, nor only to be let forth by steel—the vitals need not
be searched throughout by plunging a sword among them
to the hilt: death lies near the surface. I have not appointed
any particular spot for these blows—the body may be pierced
wherever you please. That very act which is called dying, by
which the breath of life leaves the body, is too short for you

to be able to estimate its quickness: whether a knot crushes the windpipe, or water stops your breathing: whether you fall headlong from a height and perish upon the hard ground below, or a mouthful of fire checks the drawing of your breath—whatever it is, it acts swiftly. Do you not blush to spend so long a time in dreading what takes so short a time to do?"

OF CONSOLATION

ADDRESSED TO MARCIA

1. Did I not know, Marcia, that you have as little of a woman's weakness of mind as of her other vices, and that your life was regarded as a pattern of antique virtue, I should not have dared to combat your grief, which is one that many men fondly nurse and embrace, nor should I have conceived the hope of persuading you to hold fortune blameless, having to plead for her at such an unfavorable time, before so partial a judge, and against such an odious charge. I derive confidence, however, from the proved strength of your mind, and your virtue, which has been proved by a severe test. All men know how well you behaved towards your father, whom you loved as dearly as your children in all respects, save that you did not wish him to survive you: indeed, for all that I know you may have wished that also: for great affection ventures to break some of the golden rules of life. You did all that lay in your power to avert the death of your father, Aulus Cremutius Cordus; but when it became clear that, surrounded as he was by the myrmidons of Sejanus, there was no other way of escape from slavery, you did not indeed approve of his resolution, but gave up all attempts to oppose it; you shed tears openly, and choked down your sobs, yet did not screen them behind a smiling face; and you did all this in the present century, when not to be unnatural towards one's parents is

considered the height of filial affection. When the changes of our times gave you an opportunity, you restored to the use of man that genius of your father for which he had suffered, and made him in real truth immortal by publishing as an eternal memorial of him those books which that bravest of men had written with his own blood. You have done a great service to Roman literature: a large part of Cordus's books had been burned; a great service to posterity, who will receive a true account of events, which cost its author so dear; and a great service to himself, whose memory flourishes and ever will flourish, as long as men set any value upon the facts of Roman history, as long as anyone lives who wishes to review the deeds of our fathers, to know what a true Roman was like—one who still remained unconquered when all other necks were broken in to receive the yoke of Sejanus, one who was free in every thought, feeling, and act. By Hercules, the state would have sustained a great loss if you had not brought him forth from the oblivion to which his two splendid qualities, eloquence and independence, had consigned him: he is now read, is popular, is received into men's hands and bosoms, and fears no old age: but as for those who butchered him, before long men will cease to speak even of their crimes, the only things by which they are remembered. This greatness of mind in you has forbidden me to take into consideration your sex or your face, still clouded by the sorrow by which so many years ago it was suddenly overcast. See; I shall do nothing underhand, nor try to steal away your sorrows: I have reminded you of old hurts, and to prove that your present wound may be healed, I have shown you the scar of one which was equally severe. Let others use soft measures and caresses; I have determined to do battle with your grief, and I will dry those weary and exhausted eyes, which already, to tell you the truth, are weeping more from habit than from sorrow. I will effect this cure, if possible, with your goodwill: if you disapprove of my efforts, or dislike them, then you must continue to hug and fondle the grief which you have adopted as the survivor of your son. What, I pray you, is to be the end of it? All means have been tried in vain: the consolations of your friends, who are weary of offering them, and the influence of great men who are related to you: literature, a taste which your father enjoyed and which you have inherited from him, now finds your ears closed, and affords you but a futile consolation, which scarcely engages your thoughts for a moment. Even time itself, nature's greatest remedy, which quiets the most bitter grief, loses its power with you alone. Three years have already passed, and still your grief has lost none of its first poignancy, but renews and strengthens itself day by day, and has now dwelled so long with you that it has acquired a domicile in your mind, and actually thinks that it would be base to leave it. All vices sink into our whole being, if we do not crush them before they gain a footing; and in like manner these sad, pitiable, and discordant feelings end by feeding upon their own bitterness, until the unhappy mind takes a sort of morbid delight in grief. I should have liked, therefore, to have attempted to effect this cure in the earliest stages of the disorder, before its force was fully developed; it might have been checked by milder remedies, but now that it has been confirmed by time it cannot be beaten without a hard struggle. In like manner, wounds heal easily when the blood is fresh upon them: they can then be cleared out and brought to the surface, and admit of being probed by the finger: when disease has turned them into malignant ulcers, their cure is more difficult. I cannot now influence so strong a grief by polite and mild measures: it must be broken down by force.

2. I am aware that all who wish to give anyone advice begin with precepts, and end with examples: but it is sometimes useful to alter this fashion, for we must deal differently with different people. Some are guided by reason, others must be confronted with authority and the names of celebrated persons, whose brilliancy dazzles their mind and destroys their

power of free judgment. I will place before your eyes two of the greatest examples belonging to your sex and your century: one, that of a woman who allowed herself to be entirely carried away by grief; the other, one who, though afflicted by a like misfortune, and an even greater loss, yet did not allow her sorrows to reign over her for a very long time, but quickly restored her mind to its accustomed frame. Octavia and Livia, the former Augustus's sister, the latter his wife, both lost their sons when they were young men, and when they were certain of succeeding to the throne. Octavia lost Marcellus, whom both his father-in-law and his uncle had begun to depend upon, and to place upon his shoulders the weight of the empire—a young man of keen intelligence and firm character, frugal and moderate in his desires to an extent which deserved especial admiration in one so young and so wealthy, strong to endure labour, averse to indulgence, and able to bear whatever burden his uncle might choose to lay, or I may say to pile upon his shoulders. Augustus had well chosen him as a foundation, for he would not have given way under any weight, however excessive. His mother never ceased to weep and sob during her whole life, never endured to listen to wholesome advice, never even allowed her thoughts to be diverted from her sorrow. She remained during her whole life just as she was during the funeral, with all the strength of her mind intently fixed upon one subject. I do not say that she lacked the courage to shake off her grief, but she refused to be comforted, thought that it would be a second bereavement to lose her tears, and would not have any portrait of her darling son, nor allow any allusion to be made to him. She hated all mothers, and raged against Livia with especial fury, because it seemed as though the brilliant prospect once in store for her own child was now transferred to Livia's son. Passing all her days in darkened rooms and alone, not conversing even with her brother, she refused to accept the poems which were composed in memory of Marcellus, and all the other honours paid him by literature, and closed her ears against all consolation. She lived buried and hidden from view, neglecting her accustomed duties, and actually angry with the excessive splendour of her brother's prosperity, in which she shared. Though surrounded by her children and grandchildren, she would not lay aside her mourning garb, though by retaining it she seemed to put a slight upon all her relations, in thinking herself bereaved in spite of their being alive.

3. Livia lost her son Drusus, who would have been a great emperor, and was already a great general: he had marched far into Germany, and had planted the Roman standards in places where the very existence of the Romans was hardly known. He died on the march, his very foes treating him with respect, observing a reciprocal truce, and not having the heart to wish for what would do them most service. In addition to his dying thus in his country's service, great sorrow for him was expressed by the citizens, the provinces, and the whole of Italy, through which his corpse was attended by the people of the free towns and colonies, who poured out to perform the last sad offices to him, till it reached Rome in a procession which resembled a triumph. His mother was not permitted to receive his last kiss and gather the last fond words from his dying lips: she followed the relics of her Drusus on their long journey, though every one of the funeral pyres with which all Italy was glowing seemed to renew her grief, as though she had lost him so many times. When, however, she at last laid him in the tomb, she left her sorrow there with him, and grieved no more than was becoming to a Caesar or due to a son. She did not cease to make frequent mention of the name of her Drusus, to set up his portrait in all places, both public and private, and to speak of him and listen while others spoke of him with the greatest pleasure: she lived with his memory; which none can embrace and consort with who has made it painful to himself. Choose, therefore, which of these two examples

you think the more commendable: if you prefer to follow the former, you will remove yourself from the number of the living; you will shun the sight both of other people's children and of your own, and even of him whose loss you deplore; you will be looked upon by mothers as an omen of evil; you will refuse to take part in honourable, permissible pleasures, thinking them unbecoming for one so afflicted; you will be loth to linger above ground, and will be especially angry with your age, because it will not straightaway bring your life abruptly to an end. I here put the best construction on what is really most contemptible and foreign to your character. I mean that you will show yourself unwilling to live, and unable to die. If, on the other hand, showing a milder and better regulated spirit, you try to follow the example of the latter most exalted lady, you will not be in misery, nor will you wear your life out with suffering. Plague on it! what madness this is, to punish one's self because one is unfortunate, and not to lessen, but to increase one's ills! You ought to display, in this matter also, that decent behaviour and modesty which has characterised all your life: for there is such a thing as self-restraint in grief also. You will show more respect for the youth himself, who well deserves that it should make you glad to speak and think of him, if you make him able to meet his mother with a cheerful countenance, even as he was wont to do when alive.

4. I will not invite you to practise the sterner kind of maxims, nor bid you bear the lot of humanity with more than human philosophy; neither will I attempt to dry a mother's eyes on the very day of her son's burial. I will appear with you before an arbitrator: the matter upon which we shall join issue is, whether grief ought to be deep or unceasing. I doubt not that you will prefer the example of Julia Augusta, who was your intimate friend: she invites you to follow her method: she, in her first paroxysm, when grief is especially keen and hard to bear, betook herself for consolation to Areus, her husband's

teacher in philosophy, and declared that this did her much good; more good than the thought of the Roman people, whom she was unwilling to sadden by her mourning; more than Augustus, who, staggering under the loss of one of his two chief supporters, ought not to be yet more bowed down by the sorrow of his relatives; more even than her son Tiberius, whose affection during that untimely burial of one for whom whole nations wept made her feel that she had only lost one member of her family. This was, I imagine, his introduction to and grounding in philosophy of a woman peculiarly tenacious of her own opinion:—"Even to the present day, Julia, as far as I can tell—and I was your husband's constant companion, and knew not only what all men were allowed to know, but all the most secret thoughts of your hearts—you have been careful that no one should find anything to blame in your conduct; not only in matters of importance, but even in trifles you have taken pains to do nothing which you could wish common fame, that most frank judge of the acts of princes, to overlook. Nothing, I think, is more admirable than that those who are in high places should pardon many shortcomings in others, and have to ask it for none of their own. So also in this matter of mourning you ought to act up to your maxim of doing nothing which you could wish undone, or done otherwise.

5. "In the next place, I pray and beseech you not to be self-willed and beyond the management of your friends. You must be aware that none of them know how to behave, whether to mention Drusus in your presence or not, as they neither wish to wrong a noble youth by forgetting him, nor to hurt you by speaking of him. When we leave you and assemble together by ourselves, we talk freely about his sayings and doings, treating them with the respect which they deserve: in your presence deep silence is observed about him, and thus you lose that greatest of pleasures, the hearing the praises of your son, which I doubt not you would be willing to hand

down to all future ages, had you the means of so doing, even at the cost of your own life. Wherefore endure to listen to, nay, encourage conversation of which he is the subject, and let your ears be open to the name and memory of your son. You ought not to consider this painful, like those who in such a case think that part of their misfortune consists in listening to consolation. As it is, you have altogether run into the other extreme, and, forgetting the better aspects of your lot, look only upon its worse side: you pay no attention to the pleasure you have had in your son's society and your joyful meetings with him, the sweet caresses of his babyhood, the progress of his education: you fix all your attention upon that last scene of all: and to this, as though it were not shocking enough, you add every horror you can. Do not, I implore you, take a perverse pride in appearing the most unhappy of women: and reflect also that there is no great credit in behaving bravely in times of prosperity, when life glides easily with a favouring current: neither does a calm sea and fair wind display the art of the pilot: some foul weather is wanted to prove his courage. Like him, then, do not give way, but rather plant yourself firmly, and endure whatever burden may fall upon you from above, scared though you may have been at the first roar of the tempest. There is nothing that fastens such a reproach on Fortune as resignation." After this he points out to her the son who is yet alive: he points out grandchildren from the lost one.

6. It is your trouble, Marcia, which has been dealt with here: it is beside your couch of mourning that Areus has been sitting: change the characters, and it is you whom he has been consoling. But, on the other hand, Marcia, suppose that you have sustained a greater loss than ever mother did before you: see, I am not soothing you or making light of your misfortune: if fate can be overcome by tears, let us bring tears to bear upon it: let every day be passed in mourning, every night be spent in sorrow instead of sleep: let your breast be torn by your own

hands, your very face attacked by them, and every kind of cruelty be practised by your grief, if it will profit you. But if the dead cannot be brought back to life, however much we may beat our breasts, if destiny remains fixed and immovable forever, not to be changed by any sorrow, however great, and death does not loose his hold of anything that he once has taken away, then let our futile grief be brought to an end. Let us, then, steer our own course, and no longer allow ourselves to be driven to leeward by the force of our misfortune. He is a sorry pilot who lets the waves wring his rudder from his grasp, who leaves the sails to fly loose, and abandons the ship to the storm: but he who boldly grasps the helm and clings to it until the sea closes over him, deserves praise even though he be shipwrecked.

7. "But," say you, "sorrow for the loss of one's own children is natural." Who denies it? provided it be reasonable? for we cannot help feeling a pang, and the stoutest-hearted of us are cast down not only at the death of those dearest to us, but even when they leave us on a journey. Nevertheless, the mourning which public opinion enjoins is more than nature insists upon. Observe how intense and yet how brief are the sorrows of dumb animals: we hear a cow lowing for one or two days, nor do mares pursue their wild and senseless gallops for longer: wild beasts after they have tracked their lost cubs throughout the forest, and often visited their plundered dens, quench their rage within a short space of time. Birds circle round their empty nests with loud and piteous cries, yet almost immediately resume their ordinary flight in silence; nor does any creature spend long periods in sorrowing for the loss of its offspring, except man, who encourages his own grief, the measure of which depends not upon his sufferings, but upon his will. You may know that to be utterly broken down by grief is not natural, by observing that the same bereavement inflicts a deeper wound upon women than upon men, upon savages than upon civilised and cultivated

persons, upon the unlearned than upon the learned: yet those passions which derive their force from nature are equally powerful in all men: therefore it is clear that a passion of varying strength cannot be a natural one. Fire will burn all people equally, male and female, of every rank and every age: steel will exhibit its cutting power on all bodies alike: and why? Because these things derive their strength from nature, which makes no distinction of persons. Poverty, grief, and ambition, are felt differently by different people, according as they are influenced by habit: a rooted prejudice about the terrors of these things, though they are not really to be feared, makes a man weak and unable to endure them.

8. Moreover, that which depends upon nature is not weakened by delay, but grief is gradually effaced by time. However obstinate it may be, though it be daily renewed and be exasperated by all attempts to soothe it, yet even this becomes weakened by time, which is the most efficient means of taming its fierceness. You, Marcia, have still a mighty sorrow abiding with you, nevertheless it already appears to have become blunted: it is obstinate and enduring, but not so acute as it was at first: and this also will be taken from you piecemeal by succeeding years. Whenever you are engaged in other pursuits your mind will be relieved from its burden: at present you keep watch over yourself to prevent this. Yet there is a great difference between allowing and forcing yourself to grieve. How much more in accordance with your cultivated taste it would be to put an end to your mourning instead of looking for the end to come, and not to wait for the day when your sorrow shall cease against your will: dismiss it of your own accord.

9. "Why then," you ask, "do we show such persistence in mourning for our friends, if it be not nature that bids us do so?" It is because we never expect that any evil will befall ourselves before it comes, we will not be taught by seeing the misfortunes of others that they are the common inheritance of all

men, but imagine that the path which we have begun to tread is free from them and less beset by dangers than that of other people. How many funerals pass our houses? yet we do not think of death. How many untimely deaths? we think only of our son's coming of age, of his service in the army, or of his succession to his father's estate. How many rich men suddenly sink into poverty before our very eyes, without its ever occurring to our minds that our own wealth is exposed to exactly the same risks? When, therefore, misfortune befalls us, we cannot help collapsing all the more completely, because we are struck as it were unawares: a blow which has long been foreseen falls much less heavily upon us. Do you wish to know how completely exposed you are to every stroke of fate, and that the same shafts which have transfixed others are whirling around yourself? then imagine that you are mounting without sufficient armour to assault some city wall or some strong and lofty position manned by a great host, expect a wound, and suppose that all those stones, arrows, and darts which fill the upper air are aimed at your body: whenever anyone falls at your side or behind your back, exclaim, "Fortune, you will not outwit me, or catch me confident and heedless: I know what you are preparing to do: you have struck down another, but you aimed at me." Whoever looks upon his own affairs as though he were at the point of death? which of us ever dares to think about banishment, want, or mourning? who, if advised to meditate upon these subjects, would not reject the idea like an evil omen, and bid it depart from him and alight on the heads of his enemies, or even on that of his untimely adviser? "I never thought it would happen!" How can you think that anything will not happen, when you know that it may happen to many men, and has happened to many? That is a noble verse, and worthy of a nobler source than the stage:—

What one hath suffered may befall us all.

That man has lost his children: you may lose yours. That man has been convicted: your innocence is in peril. We are deceived and weakened by this delusion, when we suffer what we never foresaw that we possibly could suffer: but by looking forward to the coming of our sorrows we take the sting out of them when they come.

10. My Marcia, all these adventitious circumstances which glitter around us, such as children, office in the state, wealth, large halls, vestibules crowded with clients seeking vainly for admittance, a noble name, a well-born or beautiful wife, and every other thing which depends entirely upon uncertain and changeful fortune, are but furniture which is not our own, but entrusted to us on loan: none of these things are given to us outright: the stage of our lives is adorned with properties gathered from various sources, and soon to be returned to their several owners: some of them will be taken away on the first day, some on the second, and but few will remain till the end. We have, therefore, no grounds for regarding ourselves with complacency, as though the things which surround us were our own: they are only borrowed: we have the use and enjoyment of them for a time regulated by the lender, who controls his own gift: it is our duty always to be able to lay our hands upon what has been lent us with no fixed date for its return, and to restore it when called upon without a murmur: the most detestable kind of debtor is he who rails at his creditor. Hence all our relatives, both those who by the order of their birth we hope will outlive ourselves, and those who themselves most properly wish to die before us, ought to be loved by us as persons whom we cannot be sure of having with us forever, nor even for long. We ought frequently to remind ourselves that we must love the things of this life as we would what is shortly to leave us, or indeed in the very act of leaving us. Whatever gift Fortune bestows upon a man, let him think while he enjoys it, that it will prove as fickle as

the goddess from whom it came. Snatch what pleasure you can from your children, allow your children in their turn to take pleasure in your society, and drain every pleasure to the dregs without any delay. We cannot reckon on to-night, nay, I have allowed too long a delay, we cannot reckon on this hour: we must make haste: the enemy presses on behind us: soon that society of yours will be broken up, that pleasant company will be taken by assault and dispersed. Pillage is the universal law: unhappy creatures, know you not that life is but a flight? If you grieve for the death of your son, the fault lies with the time when he was born, for at his birth he was told that death was his doom: it is the law under which he was born, the fate which has pursued him ever since he left his mother's womb. We have come under the dominion of Fortune, and a harsh and unconquerable dominion it is: at her caprice we must suffer all things whether we deserve them or not. She mal-treats our bodies with anger, insult, and cruelty: some she burns, the fire being sometimes applied as a punishment and sometimes as a remedy: some she imprisons, allowing it to be done at one time by our enemies, at another by our country-men: she tosses others naked on the changeful seas, and after their struggle with the waves will not even cast them out upon the sand or the shore, but will entomb them in the belly of some huge sea-monster: she wears away others to a skeleton by divers kinds of disease, and keeps them long in suspense between life and death: she is as capricious in her rewards and punishments as a fickle, whimsical, and careless mistress is with those of her slaves.

11. Why need we weep over parts of our life? the whole of it calls for tears: new miseries assail us before we have freed ourselves from the old ones. You, therefore, who allow them to trouble you to an unreasonable extent ought especially to restrain yourselves, and to muster all the powers of the human breast to combat your fears and your pains. Moreover, what forget-fulness of your own position and that of mankind is this?

You were born a mortal, and you have given birth to mortals: yourself a weak and fragile body, liable to all diseases, can you have hoped to produce anything strong and lasting from such unstable materials? Your son has died: in other words he has reached that goal towards which those whom you regard as more fortunate than your offspring are still hastening: this is the point towards which move at different rates all the crowds which are squabbling in the law courts, sitting in the theatres, praying in the temples. Those whom you love and those whom you despise will both be made equal in the same ashes. This is the meaning of that command, KNOW THYSELF, which is written on the shrine of the Pythian oracle. What is man? a potter's vessel, to be broken by the slightest shake or toss: it requires no great storm to rend you asunder: you fall to pieces wherever you strike. What is man? a weakly and frail body, naked, without any natural protection, dependent on the help of others, exposed to all the scorn of Fortune; even when his muscles are well trained he is the prey and the food of the first wild beast he meets, formed of weak and unstable substances, fair in outward feature, but unable to endure cold, heat, or labour, and yet falling to ruin if kept in sloth and idleness, fearing his very victuals, for he is starved if he has them not, and bursts if he has too much. He cannot be kept safe without anxious care, his breath only stays in the body on sufferance, and has no real hold upon it; he starts at every sudden danger, every loud and unexpected noise that reaches his ears. Ever a cause of anxiety to ourselves, diseased and useless as we are, can we be surprised at the death of a creature which can be killed by a single hiccup? Is it a great undertaking to put an end to us? why, smells, tastes, fatigue and want of sleep, food and drink, and the very necessaries of life, are mortal. Whithersoever he moves he straightaway becomes conscious of his weakness, not being able to bear all climates, falling sick after drinking strange water, breathing an air to which he is not accustomed, or from other causes and reasons of the most trifling kind, frail, sickly, entering

MINOR DIALOGUES OF SENECA

upon his life with weeping: yet nevertheless what a disturbance this despicable creature makes! what ideas it conceives,
forgetting its lowly condition! It exercises its mind upon matters which are immortal and eternal, and arranges the affairs
of its grandchildren and great-grandchildren, while death
surprises it in the midst of its far-reaching schemes, and what
we call old age is but the round of a very few years.

12. Supposing that your sorrow has any method at all, is it your
own sufferings or those of him who is gone that it has in
view? Why do you grieve over your lost son? is it because you
have received no pleasure from him, or because you would
have received more had he lived longer? If you answer that
you have received no pleasure from him you make your loss
more endurable: for men miss less when lost what has given
them no enjoyment or gladness. If, again, you admit that
you have received much pleasure, it is your duty not to complain of that part which you have lost, but to return thanks
for that which you have enjoyed. His rearing alone ought to
have brought you a sufficient return for your labours, for
it can hardly be that those who take the greatest pains to
rear puppies, birds, and such like paltry objects of amusement derive a certain pleasure from the sight and touch and
fawning caresses of these dumb creatures, and yet that those
who rear children should not find their reward in doing so.
Thus, even though his industry may have gained nothing for
you, his carefulness may have saved nothing for you, his fore-
sight may have given you no advice, yet you found sufficient
reward in having owned him and loved him. "But," say you,
"it might have lasted longer." True, but you have been better
dealt with than if you had never had a son, for, supposing you
were given your choice, which is the better lot, to be happy
for a short time or not at all? It is better to enjoy pleasures
which soon leave us than to enjoy none at all. Which, again,
would you choose? to have had one who was a disgrace to
you, and who merely filled the position and owned the name

of your son, or one of such noble character as your son's was? a youth who soon grew discreet and dutiful, soon became a husband and a father, soon became eager for public honours, and soon obtained the priesthood, winning his way to all these admirable things with equally admirable speed. It falls to scarcely anyone's lot to enjoy great prosperity, and also to enjoy it for a long time: only a dull kind of happiness can last for long and accompany us to the end of our lives. The immortal gods, who did not intend to give you a son for long, gave you one who was straightaway what another would have required long training to become. You cannot even say that you have been specially marked by the gods for misfortune because you have had no pleasure in your son. Look at any company of people, whether they be known to you or not: everywhere you will see some who have endured greater misfortunes than your own. Great generals and princes have undergone like bereavements: mythology tells us that the gods themselves are not exempt from them, its aim, I suppose, being to lighten our sorrow at death by the thought that even deities are subject to it. Look around, I repeat, at everyone: you cannot mention any house so miserable as not to find comfort in the fact of another being yet more miserable. I do not, by Hercules, think so ill of your principles as to suppose that you would bear your sorrow more lightly were I to show you an enormous company of mourners: that is a spiteful sort of consolation which we derive from the number of our fellow sufferers: nevertheless I will quote some instances, not indeed in order to teach you that this often befalls men, for it is absurd to multiply examples of man's mortality, but to let you know that there have been many who have lightened their misfortunes by patient endurance of them. I will begin with the luckiest man of all. Lucius Sulla lost his son, yet this did not impair either the spitefulness or the brilliant valour which he displayed at the expense of his enemies and his countrymen alike, nor did it make him appear to have assumed his well-known title untruly that he did so after his

son's death, fearing neither the hatred of men, by whose sufferings that excessive prosperity of his was purchased, nor
the ill will of the gods, to whom it was a reproach that Sulla
should be so truly The Fortunate. What, however, Sulla's real
character was may pass among questions still undecided:
even his enemies will admit that he took up arms with honour, and laid them aside with honour: his example proves the
point at issue, that an evil which befalls even the most prosperous cannot be one of the first magnitude.

13. That Greece cannot boast unduly of that father who, being
in the act of offering sacrifice when he heard the news of
his son's death, merely ordered the flute-player to be silent,
and removed the garland from his head, but accomplished
all the rest of the ceremony in due form, is due to a Roman,
Pulvillus the high priest. When he was in the act of holding
the doorpost and dedicating the Capitol the news of his son's
death was brought to him. He pretended not to hear it, and
pronounced the form of words proper for the high priest
on such an occasion, without his prayer being interrupted
by a single groan, begging that Jupiter would show himself
gracious, at the very instant that he heard his son's name
mentioned as dead. Do you imagine that this man's mourning knew no end, if the first day and the first shock could
not drive him, though a father, away from the public altar of
the state, or cause him to mar the ceremony of dedication
by words of ill omen? Worthy, indeed, of the most exalted
priesthood was he who ceased not to revere the gods even
when they were angry. Yet he, after he had gone home, filled
his eyes with tears, said a few words of lamentation, and per-
formed the rites with which it was then customary to honour
the dead, resumed the expression of countenance which he
had worn in the Capitol.

Paulus, about the time of his magnificent triumph, in
which he drove Perses in chains before his car, gave two of
his sons to be adopted into other families, and buried those

whom he had kept for himself. What, think you, must those whom he kept have been, when Scipio was one of those whom he gave away? It was not without emotion that the Roman people looked upon Paulus's empty chariot: nevertheless he made a speech to them, and returned thanks to the gods for having granted his prayer: for he had prayed that, if any offering to Nemesis were due in consequence of the stupendous victory which he had won, it might be paid at his own expense rather than at that of his country. Do you see how magnanimously he bore his loss? he even congratulated himself on being left childless, though who had more to suffer by such a change? he lost at once his comforters and his helpers. Yet Perses did not have the pleasure of seeing Paulus look sorrowful.

14. Why should I lead you on through the endless series of great men and pick out the unhappy ones, as though it were not more difficult to find happy ones? for how few households have remained possessed of all their members until the end? what one is there that has not suffered some loss? Take any one year you please and name the consuls for it: if you like, that of Lucius Bibulus and Gaius Caesar; you will see that, though these colleagues were each other's bitterest enemies, yet their fortunes agreed. Lucius Bibulus, a man more remarkable for goodness than for strength of character, had both his sons murdered at the same time, and even insulted by the Egyptian soldiery, so that the agent of his bereavement was as much a subject for tears as the bereavement itself. Nevertheless Bibulus, who during the whole of his year of office had remained hidden in his house, to cast reproach upon his colleague Caesar on the day following that upon which he heard of both his sons' deaths, came forth and went through the routine business of his magistracy. Who could devote less than one day to mourning for two sons? Thus soon did he end his mourning for his children, although he had mourned a whole year for his consulship. Gaius Caesar,

after having traversed Britain, and not allowed even the ocean to set bounds to his successes, heard of the death of his daughter, which hurried on the crisis of affairs. Already Gnaeus Pompeius stood before his eyes, a man who would ill endure that anyone besides himself should become a great power in the state, and one who was likely to place a check upon his advancement, which he had regarded as onerous even when each gained by the other's rise: yet within three days' time he resumed his duties as general, and conquered his grief as quickly as he was wont to conquer everything else.

15. Why need I remind you of the deaths of the other Caesars, whom fortune appears to me sometimes to have outraged in order that even by their deaths they might be useful to mankind, by proving that not even they, although they were styled "sons of gods," and "fathers of gods to come," could exercise the same power over their own fortunes which they did over those of others? The Emperor Augustus lost his children and his grandchildren, and after all the family of Caesar had perished was obliged to prop his empty house by adopting a son: yet he bore his losses as bravely as though he were already personally concerned in the honour of the gods, and as though it were especially to his interest that no one should complain of the injustice of Heaven. Tiberius Caesar lost both the son whom he begot and the son whom he adopted, yet he himself pronounced a panegyric upon his son from the Rostra, and stood in full view of the corpse, which merely had a curtain on one side to prevent the eyes of the high priest resting upon the dead body, and did not change his countenance, though all the Romans wept: he gave Sejanus, who stood by his side, a proof of how patiently he could endure the loss of his relatives. See you not what numbers of most eminent men there have been, none of whom have been spared by this blight which prostrates us all: men, too, adorned with every grace of character, and every distinction that public or private life can confer. It appears as though this plague moved

in a regular orbit, and spread ruin and desolation among us all without distinction of persons, all being alike its prey. Bid any number of individuals tell you the story of their lives: you will find that all have paid some penalty for being born.

16. I know what you will say, "You quote men as examples: you forget that it is a woman that you are trying to console." Yet who would say that nature has dealt grudgingly with the minds of women, and stunted their virtues? Believe me, they have the same intellectual power as men, and the same capacity for honourable and generous action. If trained to do so, they are just as able to endure sorrow or labour. Ye good gods, do I say this in that very city in which Lucretia and Brutus removed the yoke of kings from the necks of the Romans? We owe liberty to Brutus, but we owe Brutus to Lucretia—in which Cloelia, for the sublime courage with which she scorned both the enemy and the river, has been almost reckoned as a man. The statue of Cloelia, mounted on horseback, in that busiest of thoroughfares, the Sacred Way, continually reproaches the youth of the present day, who never mount anything but a cushioned seat in a carriage, with journeying in such a fashion through that very city in which we have enrolled even women among our knights. If you wish me to point out to you examples of women who have bravely endured the loss of their children, I shall not go far afield to search for them: in one family I can quote two Cornelias, one the daughter of Scipio, and the mother of the Gracchi, who made acknowledgment of the birth of her twelve children by burying them all: nor was it so hard to do this in the case of the others, whose birth and death were alike unknown to the public, but she beheld the murdered and unburied corpses of both Tiberius Gracchus and Gaius Gracchus, whom even those who will not call them good must admit were great men. Yet to those who tried to console her and called her unfortunate, she answered, "I shall never cease to call myself happy, because I am the mother of the Gracchi." Cornelia,

the wife of Livius Drusus, lost by the hands of an unknown assassin a young son of great distinction, who was treading in the footsteps of the Gracchi, and was murdered in his own house just when he had so many bills halfway through the process of becoming law: nevertheless she bore the untimely and unavenged death of her son with as lofty a spirit as he had shown in carrying his laws. Will you not, Marcia, forgive fortune because she has not refrained from striking you with the darts with which she launched at the Scipios, and the mothers and daughters of the Scipios, and with which she has attacked the Caesars themselves? Life is full of misfortunes; our path is beset with them: no one can make a long peace, nay, scarcely an armistice with fortune. You, Marcia, have borne four children: now they say that no dart which is hurled into a close column of soldiers can fail to hit one,— ought you then to wonder at not having been able to lead along such a company without exciting the ill will of Fortune, or suffering loss at her hands? "But," say you, "Fortune has treated me unfairly, for she not only has bereaved me of my son, but chose my best beloved to deprive me of." Yet you never can say that you have been wronged, if you divide the stakes equally with an antagonist who is stronger than yourself: Fortune has left you two daughters, and their children: she has not even taken away altogether him who you now mourn for, forgetful of his elder brother: you have two daughters by him, who if you support them ill will prove great burdens, but if well, great comforts to you. You ought to prevail upon yourself, when you see them, to let them remind you of your son, and not of your grief. When a husbandman's trees have either been torn up, roots and all, by the wind, or broken off short by the force of a hurricane, he takes care of what is left of their stock, straightaway plants seeds or cuttings in the place of those which he has lost, and in a moment—for time is as swift in repairing losses as in causing them—more flourishing trees are growing than were there before. Take, then, in the place of your Metilius these his two daughters, and by their twofold consolation lighten your single sorrow. True, human nature is so constituted as to love nothing so much as what it has lost, and our yearning after those who have been taken from us makes us judge unfairly of those who are left to us: nevertheless, if you choose to reckon up how merciful Fortune has been to you even in her anger, you will feel that you have more than enough to console you. Look at all your grandchildren, and your two daughters: and say also, Marcia:—"I should indeed be cast down, if everyone's fortune followed his deserts, and if no evil ever befell good men: but as it is I perceive that no distinction is made, and that the bad and the good are both harassed alike."

17. "Still, it is a sad thing to lose a young man whom you have brought up, just as he was becoming a defence and a pride both to his mother and to his country." No one denies that it is sad: but it is the common lot of mortals. You were born to lose others, to be lost, to hope, to fear, to destroy your own peace and that of others, to fear and yet to long for death, and, worst of all, never to know what your real position is. If you were about to journey to Syracuse, and someone were to say:—"Learn beforehand all the discomforts, and all the pleasures of your coming voyage, and then set sail. The sights which you will enjoy will be as follows: first, you will see the island itself, now separated from Italy by a narrow strait, but which, we know, once formed part of the mainland. The sea suddenly broke through, and

Sever'd Sicilia from the western shore.

Next, as you will be able to sail close to Charybdis, of which the poets have sung, you will see that greediest of whirlpools, quite smooth if no south wind be blowing, but whenever there is a gale from that quarter, sucking down ships into a huge and deep abyss. You will see the fountain of Arethusa, so famed in song, with its waters bright and pellucid to the very bottom, and pouring forth an icy stream which it either finds on the spot or else plunges it underground, conveys it thither as a separate river beneath so many seas, free from any mixture of less pure water, and there brings it again to the surface. You will see a harbour which is more sheltered than all the others in the world, whether they be natural or improved by human art for the protection of shipping; so safe, that even the most violent storms are powerless to disturb it. You will see the place where the power of Athens was broken, where that natural prison, hewn deep among precipices of rock, received so many thousands of captives: you will see the great city itself, occupying a wider site than many capitals, an extremely warm resort in winter, where not a single day passes without sunshine: but when you have observed all this, you must remember that the advantages of its winter climate are counterbalanced by a hot and pestilential summer: that here will be the tyrant Dionysius, the destroyer of freedom, of justice, and of law, who is greedy of power even after conversing with Plato, and of life even after he has been exiled; that he will burn some, flog others, and behead others for slight offences; that he will exercise his lust upon both sexes. . . . You have now heard all that can attract you thither, all that can deter you from going: now, then, either set sail or remain at home!" If, after this declaration, anybody were to say that he wished to go to Syracuse, he could blame no one but himself for what befell him there, because he would not stumble upon it unknowingly, but would have gone thither fully aware of what was before him. To everyone Nature says: "I do not deceive any person. If you choose to have children, they may be handsome, or they may be deformed; perhaps they will be born dumb. One of them may perhaps prove the saviour of his country, or perhaps its betrayer. You need not despair of their being raised to such honour that for their sake no one will dare to speak evil of you: yet remember that they may reach such a pitch of infamy as themselves to become curses to you. There is nothing to prevent their performing the last offices for you, and your panegyric being spoken by your children: but hold yourself prepared nevertheless to place a son as boy, man, or greybeard, upon the funeral pyre: for years have nothing to do with the matter, since every sort of funeral in which a parent buries his child must alike be untimely. If you still choose to rear children, after I have explained these conditions to you, you render yourself incapable of blaming the gods, for they never guaranteed anything to you."

18. You may make this simile apply to your whole entrance into life. I have explained to you what attractions and what drawbacks there would be if you were thinking of going to Syracuse: now suppose that I were to come and give you advice when you were going to be born. "You are about," I should say, "to enter a city of which both gods and men are citizens, a city which contains the whole universe, which is bound by irrevocable and eternal laws, and wherein the heavenly bodies run their unwearied courses: you will see therein innumerable twinkling stars, and the sun, whose single light pervades every place, who by his daily course marks the times of day and night, and by his yearly course makes a more equal division between summer and winter. You will see his place taken by night by the moon, who borrows at her meetings with her brother a gentle and softer light, and who at one time is invisible, at another hangs full-faced above the earth, ever waxing and waning, each phase unlike the last. You will see five stars, moving in the opposite direction to the others, stemming the whirl of the skies towards the West: on the slightest motions of these depend the fortunes of nations, and according as the aspect of the planets is auspicious or malignant, the greatest empires rise and fall: you will see with wonder the gathering clouds, the falling showers, the zigzag lightning, the crashing together of the heavens. When, sated with the wonders above, you turn your eyes towards the earth, they will be met by objects of a different yet equally admirable aspect: on one side a boundless expanse of open plains, on another

the towering peaks of lofty and snow-clad mountains: the downward course of rivers, some streams running eastward, some westward from the same source: the woods which wave even on the mountaintops, the vast forests with all the creatures that dwell therein, and the confused harmony of the birds: the variously placed cities, the nations which natural obstacles keep secluded from the world, some of whom withdraw themselves to lofty mountains, while others dwell in fear and trembling on the sloping banks of rivers: the crops which are assisted by cultivation, and the trees which bear fruit even without it: the rivers that flow gently through the meadows, the lovely bays and shores that curve inwards to form harbours: the countless islands scattered over the main, which break and spangle the seas. What of the brilliancy of stones and gems, the gold that rolls amid the sands of rushing streams, the heaven-born fires that burst forth from the midst of the earth and even from the midst of the sea; the ocean itself, that binds land to land, dividing the nations by its threefold indentations, and boiling up with mighty rage? Swimming upon its waves, making them disturbed and swelling without wind, you will see animals exceeding the size of any that belong to the land, some clumsy and requiring others to guide their movements, some swift and moving faster than the utmost efforts of rowers, some of them that drink in the waters and blow them out again to the great perils of those who sail near them: you will see here ships seeking for unknown lands: you will see that man's audacity leaves nothing unattempted, and you will yourself be both a witness and a sharer in great attempts. You will both learn and teach the arts by which men's lives are supplied with necessaries, are adorned, and are ruled: but in this same place there will be a thousand pestilences fatal to both body and mind, there will be wars and highway robberies, poisonings and shipwrecks, extremes of climate and excesses of body, untimely griefs for our dearest ones, and death for ourselves, of which we cannot tell whether it will be easy or by torture at the hands of the executioner. Now consider and weigh carefully in your own mind which you would choose. If you wish to enjoy these blessings you must pass through these pains. Do you answer that you choose to live? 'Of course.' Nay, I thought you would not enter upon that of which the least diminution causes pain. Live, then, as has been agreed on. You say, "No one has asked my opinion." Our parents' opinion was taken about us, when, knowing what the conditions of life are, they brought us into it.

19. But, to come to topics of consolation, in the first place consider if you please to what our remedies must be applied, and next, in what way. It is regret for the absence of his loved one which causes a mourner to grieve: yet it is clear that this in itself is bearable enough; for we do not weep at their being absent or intending to be absent during their lifetime, although when they leave our sight we have no more pleasure in them. What tortures us, therefore, is an idea. Now every evil is just as great as we consider it to be: we have, therefore, the remedy in our own hands. Let us suppose that they are on a journey, and let us deceive ourselves: we have sent them away, or, rather, we have sent them on in advance to a place whither we shall soon follow them. Besides this, mourners are wont to suffer from the thought, "I shall have no one to protect me, no one to avenge me when I am scorned." To use a very disreputable but very true mode of consolation, I may say that in our country the loss of children bestows more influence than it takes away, and loneliness, which used to bring the aged to ruin, now makes them so powerful that some old men have pretended to pick quarrels with their sons, have disowned their own children, and have made themselves childless by their own act. I know what you will say: "My own losses do not grieve me": and indeed a man does not deserve to be consoled if he is sorry for his son's death as he would be for that of a slave, who is capable of seeing anything in his son beyond his son's self. What then, Marcia, is it that

grieves you? is it that your son has died, or that he did not live long? If it be his having died, then you ought always to have grieved, for you always knew that he would die. Reflect that the dead suffer no evils, that all those stories which make us dread the nether world are mere fables, that he who dies need fear no darkness, no prison, no blazing streams of fire, no river of Lethe, no judgment seat before which he must appear, and that Death is such utter freedom that he need fear no more despots. All that is a phantasy of the poets, who have terrified us without a cause. Death is a release from and an end of all pains: beyond it our sufferings cannot extend: it restores us to the peaceful rest in which we lay before we were born. If any one pities the dead, he ought also to pity those who have not been born. Death is neither a good nor a bad thing, for that alone which is something can be a good or a bad thing: but that which is nothing, and reduces all things to nothing, does not hand us over to either fortune, because good and bad require some material to work upon. Fortune cannot take hold of that which Nature has let go, nor can a man be unhappy if he is nothing. Your son has passed beyond the border of the country where men are forced to labour; he has reached deep and everlasting peace. He feels no fear of want, no anxiety about his riches, no stings of lust that tears the heart in guise of pleasure: he knows no envy of another's prosperity, he is not crushed by the weight of his own; even his chaste ears are not wounded by any ribaldry: he is menaced by no disaster, either to his country or to himself. He does not hang, full of anxiety, upon the issue of events, to reap even greater uncertainty as his reward: he has at last taken up a position from which nothing can dislodge him, where nothing can make him afraid.

20. O how little do men understand their own misery, that they do not praise and look forward to death as the best discovery of Nature, whether because it hedges in happiness, or because it drives away misery: because it puts an end to the

sated weariness of old age, cuts down youth in its bloom while still full of hope of better things, or calls home childhood before the harsher stages of life are reached: it is the end of all men, a relief to many, a desire to some, and it treats none so well as those to whom it comes before they call for it. Death frees the slave though his master wills it not, it lightens the captive's chains: it leads out of prison those whom headstrong power has forbidden to quit it: it points out to exiles, whose minds and eyes are ever turned towards their own country, that it makes no difference under what people's soil one lies. When Fortune has unjustly divided the common stock, and has given over one man to another, though they were born with equal rights, Death makes them all equal. After Death no one acts any more at another's bidding: in death no man suffers any more from the sense of his low position. It is open to all: it was what your father, Marcia, longed for: it is this, I say, that renders it no misery to be born, which enables me to face the threatenings of misfortune without quailing, and to keep my mind unharmed and able to command itself. I have a last appeal. I see before me crosses not all alike, but differently made by different peoples: some hang a man head downwards, some force a stick upwards through his groin, some stretch out his arms on a forked gibbet. I see cords, scourges, and instruments of torture for each limb and each joint: but I see Death also. There are bloodthirsty enemies, there are overbearing fellow countrymen, but where they are there I see Death also. Slavery is not grievous if a man can gain his freedom by one step as soon as he becomes tired of thralldom. Life, it is thanks to Death that I hold thee so dear. Think how great a blessing is a timely death, how many have been injured by living longer than they ought. If sickness had carried off that glory and support of the empire, Gnaeus Pompeius, at Naples, he would have died the undoubted head of the Roman people, but as it was, a short extension of time cast him down from his pinnacle of fame: he beheld his legions slaughtered before his eyes: and what a sad relic of that battle, in which the Senate formed the first line, was the survival of the general. He saw his Egyptian butcher, and offered his body, hallowed by so many victories, to a guardsman's sword, although even had he been unhurt, he would have regretted his safety: for what could have been more infamous than that a Pompeius should owe his life to the clemency of a king? If Marcus Cicero had fallen at the time when he avoided those daggers which Catiline aimed equally at him and at his country, he might have died as the saviour of the commonwealth which he had set free: if his death had even followed upon that of his daughter, he might have died happy. He would not then have seen swords drawn for the slaughter of Roman citizens, the goods of the murdered divided among the murderers, that men might pay from their own purse the price of their own blood, the public auction of the consul's spoil in the civil war, the public letting-out of murder to be done, brigandage, war, pillage, hosts of Catilines. Would it not have been a good thing for Marcus Cato if the sea had swallowed him up when he was returning from Cyprus after sequestrating the king's hereditary possessions, even if that very money which he was bringing to pay the soldiers in the civil war had been lost with him? He certainly would have been able to boast that no one would dare to do wrong in the presence of Cato: as it was, the extension of his life for a very few more years forced one who was born for personal and political freedom to flee from Caesar and to become Pompeius's follower. Premature death therefore did him no evil: indeed, it put an end to the power of any evil to hurt him.

21. "Yet," say you, "he perished too soon and untimely." In the first place, suppose that he had lived to extreme old age: let him continue alive to the extreme limits of human existence: how much is it, after all? Born for a very brief space of time, we regard this life as an inn which we are soon to quit that it may be made ready for the coming guest. Do I speak of our

lives, which we know roll away incredibly fast? Reckon up the centuries of cities: you will find that even those which boast of their antiquity have not existed for long. All human works are brief and fleeting; they take up no part whatever of infinite time. Tried by the standard of the universe, we regard this earth of ours, with all its cities, nations, rivers, and seaboard as a mere point: our life occupies less than a point when compared with all time, the measure of which exceeds that of the world, for indeed the world is contained many times in it. Of what importance, then, can it be to lengthen that which, however much you add to it, will never be much more than nothing? We can only make our lives long by one expedient, that is, by being satisfied with their length: you may tell me of long-lived men, whose length of days has been celebrated by tradition, you may assign a hundred and ten years apiece to them: yet when you allow your mind to conceive the idea of eternity, there will be no difference between the shortest and the longest life, if you compare the time during which any one has been alive with that during which he has not been alive. In the next place, when he died his life was complete: he had lived as long as he needed to live: there was nothing left for him to accomplish. All men do not grow old at the same age, nor indeed do all animals: some are wearied out by life at fourteen years of age, and what is only the first stage of life with man is their extreme limit of longevity. To each man a varying length of days has been assigned: no one dies before his time, because he was not destined to live any longer than he did. Everyone's end is fixed, and will always remain where it has been placed: neither industry nor favour will move it on any further. Believe, then, that you lost him by advice: he took all that was his own,

And reached the goal allotted to his life,

so you need not burden yourself with the thought, "He might have lived longer." His life has not been cut short, nor does chance ever cut short our years: every man receives as much as was promised to him: the Fates go their own way, and neither add anything nor take away anything from what they have once promised. Prayers and endeavours are all in vain: each man will have as much life as his first day placed to his credit: from the time when he first saw the light he has entered on the path that leads to death, and is drawing nearer to his doom: those same years which were added to his youth were subtracted from his life. We all fall into this mistake of supposing that it is only old men, already in the decline of life, who are drawing near to death, whereas our first infancy, our youth, indeed every time of life leads thither. The Fates ply their own work: they take from us the consciousness of our death, and, the better to conceal its approaches, death lurks under the very names we give to life: infancy changes into boyhood, maturity swallows up the boy, old age the man; these stages themselves, if you reckon them properly, are so many losses.

22. Do you complain, Marcia, that your son did not live as long as he might have done? How do you know that it was to his advantage to live longer? whether his interest was not served by this death? Whom can you find at the present time whose fortunes are grounded on such sure foundations that they have nothing to fear in the future? All human affairs are evanescent and perishable, nor is any part of our life so frail and liable to accident as that which we especially enjoy. We ought, therefore, to pray for death when our fortune is at its best, because so great is the uncertainty and turmoil in which we live, that we can be sure of nothing but what is past. Think of your son's handsome person, which you had guarded in perfect purity among all the temptations of a voluptuous capital. Who could have undertaken to keep that clear of all diseases, so that it might preserve its beauty of form unimpaired even to old age? Think of the many taints of the mind: for fine dispositions do not always

continue to their life's end to make good the promise of their youth, but have often broken down: either extravagance, all the more shameful for being indulged in late in life, takes possession of men and makes their well-begun lives end in disgrace, or they devote their entire thoughts to the eating-house and the belly, and they become interested in nothing save what they shall eat and what they shall drink. Add to this conflagrations, falling houses, shipwrecks, the agonizing operations of surgeons, who cut pieces of bone out of men's living bodies, plunge their whole hands into their entrails, and inflict more than one kind of pain to effect the cure of shameful diseases. After these comes exile; your son was not more innocent than Rutilius: imprisonment; he was not wiser than Socrates: the piercing of one's breast by a self-inflicted wound; he was not of holier life than Cato. When you look at these examples, you will perceive that nature deals very kindly with those whom she puts speedily in a place of safety because there awaited them the payment of some such price as this for their lives. Nothing is so deceptive, nothing is so treacherous as human life; by Hercules, were it not given to men before they could form an opinion, no one would take it. Not to be born, therefore, is the happiest lot of all, and the nearest thing to this, I imagine, is that we should soon finish our strife here and be restored again to our former rest. Recall to your mind that time, so painful to you, during which Sejanus handed over your father as a present to his client Satrius Secundus: he was angry with him about something or other which he had said with too great freedom, because he was not able to keep silence and see Sejanus climbing up to take his seat upon our necks, which would have been bad enough had he been placed there by his master. He was decreed the honour of a statue, to be set up in the theatre of Pompeius, which had been burned down and was being restored by Caesar. Cordus exclaimed that "Now the theatre was really destroyed." What then? should he not burst with spite at a Sejanus being set up over the ashes of Gnaeus

Pompeius, at a faithless soldier being commemorated within the memorial of a consummate commander?

The inscription was put up: and those keen-scented hounds whom Sejanus used to feed on human blood, to make them tame towards himself and fierce to all the world beside, began to bay around their victim and even to make premature snaps at him. What was he to do? If he chose to live, he must gain the consent of Sejanus; if to die, he must gain that of his daughter; and neither of them could have been persuaded to grant it: he therefore determined to deceive his daughter, and having taken a bath in order to weaken himself still further, he retired to his bed chamber on the pretence of taking a meal there. After dismissing his slaves he threw some of the food out of the window, that he might appear to have eaten it: then he took no supper, making the excuse that he had already had enough food in his chamber. This he continued to do on the second and the third day: the fourth betrayed his condition by his bodily weakness; so, embracing you, "My dearest daughter," said he, "from whom I have never throughout your whole life concealed aught but this, I have begun my journey towards death, and have already travelled halfway thither. You cannot and you ought not to call me back." So saying he ordered all light to be excluded from the room and shut himself up in the darkness. When his determination became known there was a general feeling of pleasure at the prey being snatched out of the jaws of those ravening wolves. His prosecutors, at the instance of Sejanus, went to the judgment-seat of the consuls, complained that Cordus was dying, and begged the consuls to interpose to prevent his doing what they themselves had driven him to do; so true was it that Cordus appeared to them to be escaping: an important matter was at stake, namely, whether the accused should lose the right to die. While this point was being debated, and the prosecutors were going to attend the court a second time, he had set himself free from them. Do you see, Marcia, how suddenly evil days come upon a man?

and do you weep because one of your family could not avoid dying? one of your family was within a very little of not being allowed to die.

23. Besides the fact that everything that is future is uncertain, and the only certainty is that it is more likely to turn out ill than well, our spirits find the path to the Gods above easiest when it is soon allowed to leave the society of mankind, because it has then contracted fewest impurities to weigh it down: if set free before they become hardened worldlings, before earthly things have sunk too deep into them, they fly all the more lightly back to the place from whence they came, and all the more easily wash away the stains and defilements which they may have contracted. Great minds never love to linger long in the body: they are eager to burst its bonds and escape from it, they chafe at the narrowness of their prison, having been wont to wander through space, and from aloft in the upper air to look down with contempt upon human affairs. Hence it is that Plato declares that the wise man's mind is entirely given up to death, longs for it, contemplates it, and through his eagerness for it is always striving after things which lie beyond this life. Why, Marcia, when you saw him while yet young displaying the wisdom of age, with a mind that could rise superior to all sensual enjoyments, faultless and without a blemish, able to win riches without greediness, public office without ambition, pleasure without extravagance, did you suppose it would long be your lot to keep him safe by your side? Whatever has arrived at perfection, is ripe for dissolution. Consummate virtue flees away and betakes itself out of our sight, and those things which come to maturity in the first stage of their being do not wait for the last. The brighter a fire glows, the sooner it goes out: it lasts longer when it is made up with bad and slowly burning fuel, and shows a dull light through a cloud of smoke: its being poorly fed makes it linger all the longer. So also the more brilliant men's minds, the shorter lived they are: for

when there is no room for further growth, the end is near. Fabianus tells us, what our parents themselves have seen, that there was at Rome a boy of gigantic stature, exceeding that of a man: but he soon died, and every sensible person always said that he would soon die, for he could not live to reach the age which he had assumed before it was due. So it is: too complete maturity is a proof that destruction is near, and the end approaches when growth is over.

24. Begin to reckon his age, not by years, but by virtues: he lived long enough. He was left as a ward in the care of guardians up to his fourteenth year, and never passed out of that of his mother: when he had a household of his own he was loath to leave yours, and continued to dwell under his mother's roof, though few sons can endure to live under their father's. Though a youth whose height, beauty, and vigour of body destined him for the army, yet he refused to serve, that he might not be separated from you. Consider, Marcia, how seldom mothers who live in separate houses see their children: consider how they lose and pass in anxiety all those years during which they have sons in the army, and you will see that this time, none of which you lost, was of considerable extent: he never went out of your sight: it was under your eyes that he applied himself to the cultivation of an admirable intellect and one which would have rivalled that of his grandfather, had it not been hindered by shyness, which has concealed many men's accomplishments: though a youth of unusual beauty, and living among such throngs of women who made it their business to seduce men, he gratified the wishes of none of them, and when the effrontery of some led them so far as actually to tempt him, he blushed as deeply at having found favour in their eyes as though he had been guilty. By this holiness of life he caused himself, while yet quite a boy, to be thought worthy of the priesthood, which no doubt he owed to his mother's influence; but even his mother's influence would have had no weight if the candidate for

whom it was exerted had been unfit for the post. Dwell upon these virtues, and nurse your son as it were in your lap: now he is more at leisure to respond to your caresses, he has nothing to call him away from you, he will never be an anxiety or a sorrow to you. You have grieved at the only grief so good a son could cause you: all else is beyond the power of fortune to harm, and is full of pleasure, if only you know how to make use of your son, if you do but know what his most precious quality was. It is merely the outward semblance of your son that has perished, his likeness, and that not a very good one; he himself is immortal, and is now in a far better state, set free from the burden of all that was not his own, and left simply by himself: all this apparatus which you see about us of bones and sinews, this covering of skin, this face, these our servants the hands, and all the rest of our environment, are but chains and darkness to the soul: they overwhelm it, choke it, corrupt it, fill it with false ideas, and keep it at a distance from its own true sphere: it has to struggle continually against this burden of the flesh, lest it be dragged down and sunk by it. It ever strives to rise up again to the place from whence it was sent down on earth: there eternal rest awaits it, there it will behold what is pure and clear, in place of what is foul and turbid.

25. You need not, therefore, hasten to the burial-place of your son: that which lies there is but the worst part of him and that which gave him most trouble, only bones and ashes, which are no more parts of him than clothes or other coverings of his body. He is complete, and without leaving any part of himself behind on earth has taken wing and gone away altogether: he has tarried a brief space above us while his soul was being cleansed and purified from the vices and rust which all mortal lives must contract, and from thence he will rise to the high heavens and join the souls of the blessed: a saintly company will welcome him thither,—Scipios and Catos; and among the rest of those who have held life cheap

and set themselves free, thanks to death, albeit all there are alike akin, your father, Marcia, will embrace his grandson as he rejoices in the unwonted light, will teach him the motion of the stars which are so near to them, and introduce him with joy into all the secrets of nature, not by guesswork but by real knowledge. Even as a stranger is grateful to one who shows him the way about an unknown city, so is a searcher after the causes of what he sees in the heavens to one of his own family who can explain them to him. He will delight in gazing deep down upon the earth, for it is a delight to look from aloft at what one has left below. Bear yourself, therefore, Marcia, as though you were placed before the eyes of your father and your son, yet not such as you knew them, but far loftier beings, placed in a higher sphere. Blush, then, to do any mean or common action, or to weep for those your relatives who have been changed for the better. Free to roam through the open, boundless realms of the everliving universe, they are not hindered in their course by intervening seas, lofty mountains, impassable valleys, or the treacherous flats of the Syrtes: they find a level path everywhere, are swift and ready of motion, and are permeated in their turn by the stars and dwell together with them.

26. Imagine then, Marcia, that your father, whose influence over you was as great as yours over your son, no longer in that frame of mind in which he deplored the civil wars, or in which he forever proscribed those who would have proscribed him, but in a mood as much more joyful as his abode now is higher than of old, is saying, as he looks down from the height of heaven, "My daughter, why does this sorrow possess you for so long? why do you live in such ignorance of the truth, as to think that your son has been unfairly dealt with because he has returned to his ancestors in his prime, without decay of body or mind, leaving his family flourishing? Do you not know with what storms Fortune unsettles everything? how she proves kind and compliant to none save to those who

have the fewest possible dealings with her? Need I remind you of kings who would have been the happiest of mortals had death sooner withdrawn them from the ruin which was approaching them? or of Roman generals, whose greatness, had but a few years been taken from their lives, would have wanted nothing to render it complete? or of men of the highest distinction and noblest birth who have calmly offered their necks to the stroke of a soldier's sword? Look at your father and your grandfather: the former fell into the hands of a foreign murderer: I allowed no man to take any liberties with me, and by abstinence from food showed that my spirit was as great as my writings had represented it. Why, then, should that member of our household who died most happily of all be mourned in it the longest? We have all assembled together, and, not being plunged in utter darkness, we see that with you on earth there is nothing to be wished for, nothing grand or magnificent, but all is mean, sad, anxious, and hardly receives a fractional part of the clear light in which we dwell. I need not say that here are no frantic charges of rival armies, no fleets shattering one another, no parricides, actual or meditated, no courts where men babble over lawsuits for days together, here is nothing underhand, all hearts and minds are open and unveiled, our life is public and known to all, and that we command a view of all time and of things to come. I used to take pleasure in compiling the history of what took place in one century among a few people in the most out-of-the-way corner of the world: here I enjoy the spectacle of all the centuries, the whole chain of events from age to age as long as years have been. I may view kingdoms when they rise and when they fall, and behold the ruin of cities and the new channels made by the sea. If it will be any consolation to you in your bereavement to know that it is the common lot of all, be assured that nothing will continue to stand in the place in which it now stands, but that time will lay everything low and bear it away with itself: it will sport, not only with men—for how small a part are they of the dominion of Fortune? —but with districts, provinces, quarters of the world: it will efface entire mountains, and in other places will pile new rocks on high: it will dry up seas, change the course of rivers, destroy the intercourse of nation with nation, and break up the communion and fellowship of the human race: in other regions it will swallow up cities by opening vast chasms in the earth, will shake them with earthquakes, will breathe forth pestilence from the nether world, cover all habitable ground with inundations and destroy every creature in the flooded world, or burn up all mortals by a huge conflagration. When the time shall arrive for the world to be brought to an end, that it may begin its life anew, all the forces of nature will perish in conflict with one another, the stars will be dashed together, and all the lights which now gleam in regular order in various parts of the sky will then blaze in one fire with all their fuel burning at once. Then we also, the souls of the blessed and the heirs of eternal life, whenever God thinks fit to reconstruct the universe, when all things are settling down again, we also, being a small accessory to the universal wreck, shall be changed into our old elements. Happy is your son, Marcia, in that he already knows this."

OF PEACE OF MIND

ADDRESSED TO SERENUS

1.   [*Serenus.*] When I examine myself, Seneca, some vices appear
     on the surface, and so that I can lay my hands upon them,
     while others are less distinct and harder to reach, and some
     are not always present, but recur at intervals: and these I
     should call the most troublesome, being like a roving enemy
     that assails one when he sees his opportunity, and who will
     neither let one stand on one's guard as in war, nor yet take
     one's rest without fear as in peace. The position in which I
     find myself more especially (for why should I not tell you the
     truth as I would to a physician), is that of neither being thor-
     oughly set free from the vices which I fear and hate, nor yet
     quite in bondage to them: my state of mind, though not the
     worst possible, is a particularly discontented and sulky one:
     I am neither ill nor well. It is of no use for you to tell me that
     all virtues are weakly at the outset, and that they acquire
     strength and solidity by time, for I am well aware that even
     those which do but help our outward show, such as grandeur,
     a reputation for eloquence, and everything that appeals to
     others, gain power by time. Both those which afford us real
     strength and those which do but trick us out in a more attrac-
     tive form, require long years before they gradually are
     adapted to us by time. But I fear that custom, which confirms
     most things, implants this vice more and more deeply in me.

Long acquaintance with both good and bad people leads one to esteem them all alike. What this state of weakness really is, when the mind halts between two opinions without any strong inclination towards either good or evil, I shall be better able to show you piecemeal than all at once. I will tell you what befalls me, you must find out the name of the disease. I have to confess the greatest possible love of thrift: I do not care for a bed with gorgeous hangings, nor for clothes brought out of a chest, or pressed under weights and made glossy by frequent manglings, but for common and cheap ones, that require no care either to keep them or to put them on. For food I do not want what needs whole troops of servants to prepare it and admire it, nor what is ordered many days before and served up by many hands, but something handy and easily come at, with nothing far-fetched or costly about it, to be had in every part of the world, burdensome neither to one's fortune nor one's body, not likely to go out of the body by the same path by which it came in. I like a rough and unpolished homebred servant, I like my servant born in my house: I like my country-bred father's heavy silver plate stamped with no maker's name: I do not want a table that is beauteous with dappled spots, or known to all the town by the number of fashionable people to whom it has successively belonged, but one which stands merely for use, and which causes no guest's eye to dwell upon it with pleasure or to kindle at it with envy. While I am well satisfied with this, I am reminded of the clothes of a certain schoolboy, dressed with no ordinary care and splendour, of slaves bedecked with gold and a whole regiment of glittering attendants. I think of houses too, where one treads on precious stones, and where valuables lie about in every corner, where the very roof is brilliantly painted, and a whole nation attends and accompanies an inheritance on the road to ruin. What shall I say of waters, transparent to the very bottom, which flow round the guests, and banquets worthy of the theatre in which they take place? Coming as I do from a long course of dull thrift, I find myself surrounded by the most brilliant luxury, which echoes around me on every side: my sight becomes a little dazzled by it: I can lift up my heart against it more easily than my eyes. When I return from seeing it I am a sadder, though not a worse man, I cannot walk amid my own paltry possessions with so lofty a step as before, and silently there steals over me a feeling of vexation, and a doubt whether that way of life may not be better than mine. None of these things alter my principles, yet all of them disturb me. At one time I would obey the maxims of our school and plunge into public life, I would obtain office and become consul, not because the purple robe and lictor's axes attract me, but in order that I may be able to be of use to my friends, my relatives, to all my countrymen, and indeed to all mankind. Ready and determined, I follow the advice of Zeno, Cleanthes, and Chrysippus, all of whom bid one take part in public affairs, though none of them ever did so himself: and then, as soon as something disturbs my mind, which is not used to receiving shocks, as soon as something occurs which is either disgraceful, such as often occurs in all men's lives, or which does not proceed quite easily, or when subjects of very little importance require me to devote a great deal of time to them, I go back to my life of leisure, and, just as even tired cattle go faster when they are going home, I wish to retire and pass my life within the walls of my house. "No one," I say, "that will give me no compensation worth such a loss shall ever rob me of a day. Let my mind be contained within itself and improve itself: let it take no part with other men's affairs, and do nothing which depends on the approval of others: let me enjoy a tranquillity undisturbed by either public or private troubles." But whenever my spirit is roused by reading some brave words, or some noble example spurs me into action, I want to rush into the law courts, to place my voice at one man's disposal, my services at another's, and to try to help him even though I may not succeed, or to quell the pride of some lawyer who is puffed up by ill-deserved success: but I think, by Hercules, that in philosophical speculation it is better to view things as they are, and to speak of them on their own account, and as for words, to trust to things for them, and to let one's speech simply follow whither they lead. "Why do you want to construct a fabric that will endure for ages? Do you not wish to do this in order that posterity may talk of you: yet you were born to die, and a silent death is the least wretched. Write something therefore in a simple style, merely to pass the time, for your own use, and not for publication. Less labour is needed when one does not look beyond the present." Then again, when the mind is elevated by the greatness of its thoughts, it becomes ostentatious in its use of words, the loftier its aspirations, the more loftily it desires to express them, and its speech rises to the dignity of its subject. At such times I forget my mild and moderate determination and soar higher than is my wont, using a language that is not my own. Not to multiply examples, I am in all things attended by this weakness of a well-meaning mind, to whose level I fear that I shall be gradually brought down, or, what is even more worrying, that I may always hang as though about to fall, and that there may be more the matter with me than I myself perceive: for we take a friendly view of our own private affairs, and partiality always obscures our judgment. I fancy that many men would have arrived at wisdom had they not believed themselves to have arrived there already, had they not purposely deceived themselves as to some parts of their character, and passed by others with their eyes shut: for you have no grounds for supposing that other people's flattery is more ruinous to us than our own. Who dares to tell himself the truth? Who is there, by however large a troop of caressing courtiers he may be surrounded, who in spite of them is not his own greatest flatterer? I beg you, therefore, if you have any remedy by which you could stop this vacillation of mine, to deem me worthy to owe my peace of mind to you. I am well aware that these oscillations of mind are not perilous and that they threaten me with no serious disorder: to express what I

complain of by an exact simile, I am not suffering from a
storm, but from sea-sickness. Take from me, then, this evil,
whatever it may be, and help one who is in distress within
sight of land.

2. [*Seneca.*] I have long been silently asking myself, my friend
Serenus, to what I should liken such a condition of mind, and
I find that nothing more closely resembles it than the conduct of those who, after having recovered from a long and
serious illness, occasionally experience slight touches and
twinges, and, although they have passed through the final
stages of the disease, yet have suspicions that it has not left
them, and though in perfect health yet hold out their pulse
to be felt by the physician, and whenever they feel warm sus-
pect that the fever is returning. Such men, Serenus, are not
unhealthy, but they are not accustomed to being healthy; just
as even a quiet sea or lake nevertheless displays a certain
amount of ripple when its waters are subsiding after a storm.
What you need, therefore, is not any of those harsher remedies to which allusion has been made, not that you should in
some cases check yourself, in others be angry with yourself,
in others sternly reproach yourself, but that you should adopt
that which comes last in the list, have confidence in yourself,
and believe that you are proceeding on the right path, without being led aside by the numerous divergent tracks of
wanderers which cross it in every direction, some of them circling about the right path itself. What you desire, to be
undisturbed, is a great thing, nay, the greatest thing of all,
and one which raises a man almost to the level of a god. The
Greeks call this calm steadiness of mind *euthymia*, and
Democritus's treatise upon it is excellently written: I call it
peace of mind: for there is no necessity for translating so
exactly as to copy the words of the Greek idiom: the essential
point is to mark the matter under discussion by a name which
ought to have the same meaning as its Greek name, though
perhaps not the same form. What we are seeking, then, is

how the mind may always pursue a steady, unruffled course, may be pleased with itself, and look with pleasure upon its surroundings, and experience no interruption of this joy, but abide in a peaceful condition without being ever either elated or depressed: this will be "peace of mind." Let us now consider in a general way how it may be attained: then you may apply as much as you choose of the universal remedy to your own case. Meanwhile we must drag to light the entire disease, and then each one will recognize his own part of it: at the same time you will understand how much less you suffer by your self-depreciation than those who are bound by some showy declaration which they have made, and are oppressed by some grand title of honour, so that shame rather than their own free will forces them to keep up the pretence. The same thing applies both to those who suffer from fickleness and continual changes of purpose, who always are fondest of what they have given up, and those who merely yawn and dawdle: add to these those who, like bad sleepers, turn from side to side, and settle themselves first in one manner and then in another, until at last they find rest through sheer weariness: in forming the habits of their lives they often end by adopting some to which they are not kept by any dislike of change, but in the practice of which old age, which is slow to alter, has caught them living: add also those who are by no means fickle, yet who must thank their dullness, not their consistency for being so, and who go on living not in the way they wish, but in the way they have begun to live. There are other special forms of this disease without number, but it has but one effect, that of making people dissatisfied with themselves. This arises from a distemperature of mind and from desires which one is afraid to express or unable to fulfil, when men either dare not attempt as much as they wish to do, or fail in their efforts and depend entirely upon hope: such people are always fickle and changeable, which is a necessary consequence of living in a state of suspense: they take any way to arrive at their ends, and teach and force themselves to use both dishonourable and difficult means to do so, so that when their toil has been in vain they are made wretched by the disgrace of failure, and do not regret having longed for what was wrong, but having longed for it in vain. They then begin to feel sorry for what they have done, and afraid to begin again, and their mind falls by degrees into a state of endless vacillation, because they can neither command nor obey their passions, of hesitation, because their life cannot properly develop itself, and of decay, as the mind becomes stupefied by disappointments. All these symptoms become aggravated when their dislike of a laborious misery has driven them to idleness and to secret studies, which are unendurable to a mind eager to take part in public affairs, desirous of action, and naturally restless, because, of course, it finds too few resources within itself: when therefore it loses the amusement which business itself affords to busy men, it cannot endure home, loneliness, or the walls of a room, and regards itself with dislike when left to itself. Hence arises that weariness and dissatisfaction with oneself, that tossing to and fro of a mind which can nowhere find rest, that unhappy and unwilling endurance of enforced leisure. In all cases where one feels ashamed to confess the real cause of one's suffering, and where modesty leads one to drive one's sufferings inward, the desires pent up in a little space without any vent choke one another. Hence comes melancholy and drooping of spirit, and a thousand waverings of the unsteadfast mind, which is held in suspense by unfulfilled hopes, and saddened by disappointed ones: hence comes the state of mind of those who loathe their idleness, complain that they have nothing to do, and view the progress of others with the bitterest jealousy: for an unhappy sloth favours the growth of envy, and men who cannot succeed themselves wish everyone else to be ruined. This dislike of other men's progress and despair of one's own produces a mind angered against fortune, addicted to complaining of the age in which it lives, to retiring into corners and brooding over its misery, until it becomes sick and weary of itself: for the human mind is naturally nimble and apt at movement: it delights in every opportunity of excitement and forgetfulness of itself, and the worse a man's disposition, the more he delights in this, because he likes to wear himself out with busy action, just as some sores long for the hands that injure them and delight in being touched, and the foul itch enjoys anything that scratches it. Similarly I assure you that these minds, over which desires have spread like evil ulcers, take pleasure in toils and troubles, for there are some things which please our body while at the same time they give it a certain amount of pain, such as turning oneself over and changing one's side before it is wearied, or cooling oneself in one position after another. It is like Homer's Achilles, lying first upon its face, then upon its back, placing itself in various attitudes, and, as sick people are wont, enduring none of them for long, and using changes as though they were remedies. Hence men undertake aimless wanderings, travel along distant shores, and at one time at sea, at another by land, try to soothe that fickleness of disposition which always is dissatisfied with the present. "Now let us make for Campania: now I am sick of rich cultivation: let us see wild regions, let us thread the passes of Bruttii and Lucania: yet amid this wilderness one wants something of beauty to relieve our pampered eyes after so long dwelling on savage wastes: let us seek Tarentum with its famous harbour, its mild winter climate, and its district, rich enough to support even the great hordes of ancient times. Let us now return to town: our ears have too long missed its shouts and noise: it would be pleasant also to enjoy the sight of human bloodshed." Thus one journey succeeds another, and one sight is changed for another. As Lucretius says:—

Thus every mortal from himself doth flee;

but what does he gain by so doing if he does not escape from himself? he follows himself and weighs himself down by his

own most burdensome companionship. We must understand, therefore, that what we suffer from is not the fault of
the places but of ourselves: we are weak when there is anything to be endured, and cannot support either labour or
pleasure, either one's own business or anyone else's for long.
This has driven some men to death, because by frequently
altering their purpose they were always brought back to the
same point, and had left themselves no room for anything
new. They had become sick of life and of the world itself,
and as all indulgences palled upon them they began to ask
themselves the question, "How long are we to go on doing
the same thing?"

3. You ask me what I think we had better make use of to help us
to support this ennui. "The best thing," as Athenodorus says,
"is to occupy oneself with business, with the management of
affairs of state and the duties of a citizen: for as some pass the
day in exercising themselves in the sun and in taking care of
their bodily health, and athletes find it most useful to spend
the greater part of their time in feeding up the muscles and
strength to whose cultivation they have devoted their lives;
so too for you who are training your mind to take part in the
struggles of political life, it is far more honourable to be thus
at work than to be idle. He whose object is to be of service to
his countrymen and to all mortals, exercises himself and does
good at the same time when he is engrossed in business and
is working to the best of his ability both in the interests of
the public and of private men. But," continues he, "because
innocence is hardly safe among such furious ambitions and
so many men who turn one aside from the right path, and
it is always sure to meet with more hindrance than help, we
ought to withdraw ourselves from the Forum and from public
life, and a great mind even in a private station can find room
wherein to expand freely. Confinement in dens restrains the
springs of lions and wild creatures, but this does not apply to
human beings, who often effect the most important works

in retirement. Let a man, however, withdraw himself only in such a fashion that wherever he spends his leisure his wish may still be to benefit individual men and mankind alike, both with his intellect, his voice, and his advice. The man that does good service to the state is not only he who brings forward candidates for public office, defends accused persons, and gives his vote on questions of peace and war, but he who encourages young men in well-doing, who supplies the present dearth of good teachers by instilling into their minds the principles of virtue, who seizes and holds back those who are rushing wildly in pursuit of riches and luxury, and, if he does nothing else, at least checks their course— such a man does service to the public though in a private station. Which does the most good, he who decides between foreigners and citizens (as praetor peregrinus), or, as praetor urbanus, pronounces sentence to the suitors in his court at his assistant's dictation, or he who shows them what is meant by justice, filial feeling, endurance, courage, contempt of death and knowledge of the gods, and how much a man is helped by a good conscience? If then you transfer to philosophy the time which you take away from the public service, you will not be a deserter or have refused to perform your proper task. A soldier is not merely one who stands in the ranks and defends the right or the left wing of the army, but he also who guards the gates—a service which, though less dangerous, is no sinecure—who keeps watch, and takes charge of the arsenal: though all these are bloodless duties, yet they count as military service. As soon as you have devoted yourself to philosophy, you will have overcome all disgust at life: you will not wish for darkness because you are weary of the light, nor will you be a trouble to yourself and useless to others: you will acquire many friends, and all the best men will be attracted towards you: for virtue, in however obscure a position, cannot be hidden, but gives signs of its presence: anyone who is worthy will trace it out by its footsteps: but if we give up all society, turn our backs upon the whole human race, and live

communing with ourselves alone, this solitude without any
interesting occupation will lead to a want of something to do:
we shall begin to build up and to pull down, to dam out the
sea, to cause waters to flow through natural obstacles, and
generally to make a bad disposal of the time which Nature
has given us to spend: some of us use it grudgingly, others
wastefully; some of us spend it so that we can show a profit
and loss account, others so that they have no assets remaining: than which nothing can be more shameful. Often a man
who is very old in years has nothing beyond his age by which
he can prove that he has lived a long time."

4. To me, my dearest Serenus, Athenodorus seems to have
yielded too completely to the times, to have fled too soon: I
will not deny that sometimes one must retire, but one ought
to retire slowly, at a foot's pace, without losing one's ensigns
or one's honour as a soldier: those who make terms with
arms in their hands are more respected by their enemies and
more safe in their hands. This is what I think ought to be
done by virtue and by one who practises virtue: if Fortune get
the upper hand and deprive him of the power of action, let
him not straightaway turn his back to the enemy, throw away
his arms, and run away seeking for a hiding-place, as if there
were any place whither Fortune could not pursue him, but let
him be more sparing in his acceptance of public office, and
after due deliberation discover some means by which he can
be of use to the state. He is not able to serve in the army: then
let him become a candidate for civic honours: must he live
in a private station? then let him be an advocate: is he condemned to keep silence? then let him help his countrymen
with silent counsel. Is it dangerous for him even to enter the
Forum? then let him prove himself a good comrade, a faithful friend, a sober guest in people's houses, at public shows,
and at wine-parties. Suppose that he has lost the status of
a citizen; then let him exercise that of a man: our reason
for magnanimously refusing to confine ourselves within the

walls of one city, for having gone forth to enjoy intercourse with all lands and for professing ourselves to be citizens of the world is that we may thus obtain a wider theatre on which to display our virtue. Is the bench of judges closed to you, are you forbidden to address the people from the hustings, or to be a candidate at elections? then turn your eyes away from Rome, and see what a wide extent of territory, what a number of nations present themselves before you. Thus, it is never possible for so many outlets to be closed against your ambition that more will not remain open to it: but see whether the whole prohibition does not arise from your own fault. You do not choose to direct the affairs of the state except as consul or prytanis or meddix or sufes: what should we say if you refused to serve in the army save as general or military tribune? Even though others may form the first line, and your lot may have placed you among the veterans of the third, do your duty there with your voice, encouragement, example, and spirit: even though a man's hands be cut off, he may find means to help his side in a battle, if he stands his ground and cheers on his comrades. Do something of that sort yourself: if Fortune removes you from the front rank, stand your ground nevertheless and cheer on your comrades, and if somebody stops your mouth, stand nevertheless and help your side in silence. The services of a good citizen are never thrown away: he does good by being heard and seen, by his expression, his gestures, his silent determination, and his very walk. As some remedies benefit us by their smell as well as by their taste and touch, so virtue even when concealed and at a distance sheds usefulness around. Whether she moves at her ease and enjoys her just rights, or can only appear abroad on sufferance and is forced to shorten sail to the tempest, whether it be unemployed, silent, and pent up in a narrow lodging, or openly displayed, in whatever guise she may appear, she always does good. What? do you think that the example of one who can rest nobly has no value? It is by far the best plan, therefore, to mingle leisure with business, whenever chance impediments or the state of public affairs forbid one's leading an active life: for one is never so cut off from all pursuits as to find no room left for honourable action.

5. Could you anywhere find a more miserable city than that of Athens when it was being torn to pieces by the thirty tyrants? they slew thirteen hundred citizens, all the best men, and did not leave off because they had done so, but their cruelty became stimulated by exercise. In the city which possessed that most reverend tribunal, the Court of the Areopagus, which possessed a Senate, and a popular assembly which was like a Senate, there met daily a wretched crew of butchers, and the unhappy Senate House was crowded with tyrants. A state, in which there were so many tyrants that they would have been enough to form a bodyguard for one, might surely have rested from the struggle; it seemed impossible for men's minds even to conceive hopes of recovering their liberty, nor could they see any room for a remedy for such a mass of evil: for whence could the unhappy state obtain all the Harmodiuses it would need to slay so many tyrants? Yet Socrates was in the midst of the city, and consoled its mourning Fathers, encouraged those who despaired of the republic, by his reproaches brought rich men, who feared that their wealth would be their ruin, to a tardy repentance of their avarice, and moved about as a great example to those who wished to imitate him, because he walked a free man in the midst of thirty masters. However, Athens herself put him to death in prison, and Freedom herself could not endure the freedom of one who had treated a whole band of tyrants with scorn: you may know, therefore, that even in an oppressed state a wise man can find an opportunity for bringing himself to the front, and that in a prosperous and flourishing one wanton insolence, jealousy, and a thousand other cowardly vices bear sway. We ought, therefore, to expand or contract ourselves according as the state presents itself to us, or as Fortune offers us opportunities: but in any case we

ought to move and not to become frozen still by fear: nay, he is the best man who, though peril menaces him on every side and arms and chains beset his path, nevertheless neither impairs nor conceals his virtue: for to keep oneself safe does not mean to bury oneself. I think that Curius Dentatus spoke truly when he said that he would rather be dead than alive: the worst evil of all is to leave the ranks of the living before one dies: yet it is your duty, if you happen to live in an age when it is not easy to serve the state, to devote more time to leisure and to literature. Thus, just as though you were making a perilous voyage, you may from time to time put into harbour, and set yourself free from public business without waiting for it to do so.

6.   We ought, however, first to examine our own selves, next the business which we propose to transact, next those for whose sake or in whose company we transact it.

It is above all things necessary to form a true estimate of oneself, because as a rule we think that we can do more than we are able: one man is led too far through confidence in his eloquence, another demands more from his estate than it can produce, another burdens a weakly body with some toilsome duty. Some men are too shamefaced for the conduct of public affairs, which require an unblushing front: some men's obstinate pride renders them unfit for courts: some cannot control their anger, and break into unguarded language on the slightest provocation: some cannot rein in their wit or resist making risky jokes: for all these men leisure is better than employment: a bold, haughty, and impatient nature ought to avoid anything that may lead it to use a freedom of speech which will bring it to ruin. Next we must form an estimate of the matter which we mean to deal with, and compare our strength with the deed we are about to attempt: for the bearer ought always to be more powerful than his load: indeed, loads which are too heavy for their bearer must of necessity crush him: some affairs also are not so important in themselves as they are prolific and lead to much more business, which employments, as they involve us in new and various forms of work, ought to be refused. Neither should you engage in anything from which you are not free to retreat: apply yourself to something which you can finish, or at any rate can hope to finish: you had better not meddle with those operations which grow in importance, while they are being transacted, and which will not stop where you intended them to stop.

7. In all cases one should be careful in one's choice of men, and see whether they be worthy of our bestowing a part of our life upon them, or whether we shall waste our own time and theirs also: for some even consider us to be in their debt because of our services to them. Athenodorus said that "he would not so much as dine with a man who would not be grateful to him for doing so": meaning, I imagine, that much less would he go to dinner with those who recompense the services of their friends by their table, and regard courses of dishes as donatives, as if they overrate themselves to do honour to others. Take away from these men their witnesses and spectators: they will take no pleasure in solitary gluttony. You must decide whether your disposition is better suited for vigorous action or for tranquil speculation and contemplation, and you must adopt whichever the bent of your genius inclines you for. Isocrates laid hands upon Ephorus and led him away from the Forum, thinking that he would be more usefully employed in compiling chronicles; for no good is done by forcing one's mind to engage in uncongenial work: it is vain to struggle against Nature. Yet nothing delights the mind so much as faithful and pleasant friendship: what a blessing it is when there is one whose breast is ready to receive all your secrets with safety, whose knowledge of your actions you fear less than your own conscience, whose conversation removes your anxieties, whose advice assists your plans, whose cheerfulness dispels your gloom, whose very

sight delights you! We should choose for our friends men who are, as far as possible, free from strong desires: for vices are contagious, and pass from a man to his neighbour, and injure those who touch them. As, therefore, in times of pestilence we have to be careful not to sit near people who are infected and in whom the disease is raging, because by so doing, we shall run into danger and catch the plague from their very breath; so, too, in choosing our friends' dispositions, we must take care to select those who are as far as may be unspotted by the world; for the way to breed disease is to mix what is sound with what is rotten. Yet I do not advise you to follow after or draw to yourself no one except a wise man: for where will you find him whom for so many centuries we have sought in vain? in the place of the best possible man, take him who is least bad. You would hardly find any time that would have enabled you to make a happier choice than if you could have sought for a good man from among the Platos and Xenophons and the rest of the produce of the brood of Socrates, or if you had been permitted to choose one from the age of Cato: an age which bore many men worthy to be born in Cato's time (just as it also bore many men worse than were ever known before, planners of the blackest crimes: for it needed both classes in order to make Cato understood: it wanted both good men, that he might win their approbation, and bad men, against whom he could prove his strength): but at the present day, when there is such a dearth of good men, you must be less squeamish in your choice. Above all, however, avoid dismal men who grumble at whatever happens, and find something to complain of in everything. Though he may continue loyal and friendly towards you, still one's peace of mind is destroyed by a comrade whose mind is soured and who meets every incident with a groan.

8. Let us now pass on to the consideration of property, that most fertile source of human sorrows: for if you compare all the other ills from which we suffer—deaths, sicknesses,

fears, regrets, endurance of pains and labours—with those miseries which our money inflicts upon us, the latter will far outweigh all the others. Reflect, then, how much less a grief it is never to have had any money than to have lost it: we shall thus understand that the less poverty has to lose, the less torment it has with which to afflict us: for you are mistaken if you suppose that the rich bear their losses with greater spirit than the poor: a wound causes the same amount of pain to the greatest and the smallest body. It was a neat saying of Bion's, "that it hurts bald men as much as hairy men to have their hairs pulled out": you may be assured that the same thing is true of rich and poor people, that their suffering is equal: for their money clings to both classes, and cannot be torn away without their feeling it: yet it is more endurable, as I have said, and easier not to gain property than to lose it, and therefore you will find that those upon whom Fortune has never smiled are more cheerful than those whom she has deserted. Diogenes, a man of infinite spirit, perceived this, and made it impossible that anything should be taken from him. Call this security from loss poverty, want, necessity, or any contemptuous name you please: I shall consider such a man to be happy, unless you find me another who can lose nothing. If I am not mistaken, it is a royal attribute among so many misers, sharpers, and robbers, to be the one man who cannot be injured. If anyone doubts the happiness of Diogenes, he would doubt whether the position of the immortal gods was one of sufficient happiness, because they have no farms or gardens, no valuable estates let to strange tenants, and no large loans in the money market. Are you not ashamed of yourself, you who gaze upon riches with astonished admiration? Look upon the universe: you will see the gods quite bare of property, and possessing nothing though they give everything. Do you think that this man who has stripped himself of all fortuitous accessories is a pauper, or one like to the immortal gods? Do you call Demetrius, Pompeius's freedman, a happier man, he who was not ashamed to be richer than Pompeius, who was daily furnished with a list of the number of his slaves, as a general is with that of his army, though he had long deserved that all his riches should consist of a pair of underlings, and a roomier cell than the other slaves? But Diogenes's only slave ran away from him, and when he was pointed out to Diogenes, he did not think him worth fetching back. "It is a shame," he said, "that Manes should be able to live without Diogenes, and that Diogenes should not be able to live without Manes." He seems to me to have said, "Fortune, mind your own business: Diogenes has nothing left that belongs to you. Did my slave run away? nay, he went away from me as a free man." A household of slaves requires food and clothing: the bellies of so many hungry creatures have to be filled: we must buy raiment for them, we must watch their most thievish hands, and we must make use of the services of people who weep and execrate us. How far happier is he who is indebted to no man for anything except for what he can deprive himself of with the greatest ease! Since we, however, have not such strength of mind as this, we ought at any rate to diminish the extent of our property, in order to be less exposed to the assaults of fortune: those men whose bodies can be within the shelter of their armour, are more fitted for war than those whose huge size everywhere extends beyond it, and exposes them to wounds: the best amount of property to have is that which is enough to keep us from poverty, and which yet is not far removed from it.

9. We shall be pleased with this measure of wealth if we have previously taken pleasure in thrift, without which no riches are sufficient, and with which none are insufficient, especially as the remedy is always at hand, and poverty itself by calling in the aid of thrift can convert itself into riches. Let us accustom ourselves to set aside mere outward show, and to measure things by their uses, not by their ornamental trappings: let our hunger be tamed by food, our thirst quenched

by drinking, our lust confined within needful bounds; let us learn to use our limbs, and to arrange our dress and way of life according to what was approved of by our ancestors, not in imitation of new-fangled models: let us learn to increase our continence, to repress luxury, to set bounds to our pride, to assuage our anger, to look upon poverty without prejudice, to practise thrift, albeit many are ashamed to do so, to apply cheap remedies to the wants of nature, to keep all undisciplined hopes and aspirations as it were under lock and key, and to make it our business to get our riches from ourselves and not from Fortune. We never can so thoroughly defeat the vast diversity and malignity of misfortune with which we are threatened as not to feel the weight of many gusts if we offer a large spread of canvas to the wind: we must draw our affairs into a small compass, to make the darts of Fortune of no avail. For this reason, sometimes slight mishaps have turned into remedies, and more serious disorders have been healed by slighter ones. When the mind pays no attention to good advice, and cannot be brought to its senses by milder measures, why should we not think that its interests are being served by poverty, disgrace, or financial ruin being applied to it? one evil is balanced by another. Let us then teach ourselves to be able to dine without all Rome to look on, to be the slaves of fewer slaves, to get clothes which fulfil their original purpose, and to live in a smaller house. The inner curve is the one to take, not only in running races and in the contests of the circus, but also in the race of life; even literary pursuits, the most becoming thing for a gentleman to spend money upon, are only justifiable as long as they are kept within bounds. What is the use of possessing numberless books and libraries, whose titles their owner can hardly read through in a lifetime? A student is overwhelmed by such a mass, not instructed, and it is much better to devote yourself to a few writers than to skim through many. Forty thousand books were burned at Alexandria: some would have praised this library as a most noble memorial of royal wealth, like

Titus Livius, who says that it was "a splendid result of the taste and attentive care of the kings." It had nothing to do with taste or care, but was a piece of learned luxury, nay, not even learned, since they amassed it, not for the sake of learning, but to make a show, like many men who know less about letters than a slave is expected to know, and who uses his books not to help him in his studies but to ornament his dining-room. Let a man, then, obtain as many books as he wants, but none for show. "It is more respectable," say you, "to spend one's money on such books than on vases of Corinthian brass and paintings." Not so: everything that is carried to excess is wrong. What excuses can you find for a man who is eager to buy bookcases of ivory and citrus wood, to collect the works of unknown or discredited authors, and who sits yawning amid so many thousands of books, whose backs and titles please him more than any other part of them? Thus in the houses of the laziest of men you will see the works of all the orators and historians stacked upon bookshelves reaching right up to the ceiling. At the present day a library has become as necessary an appendage to a house as a hot and cold bath. I would excuse them straightaway if they really were carried away by an excessive zeal for literature; but as it is, these costly works of sacred genius, with all the illustrations that adorn them, are merely bought for display and to serve as wall-furniture.

10. Suppose, however, that your life has become full of trouble, and that without knowing what you were doing you have fallen into some snare which either public or private Fortune has set for you, and that you can neither untie it nor break it: then remember that fettered men suffer much at first from the burdens and clogs upon their legs: afterwards, when they have made up their minds not to fret themselves about them, but to endure them, necessity teaches them to bear them bravely, and habit to bear them easily. In every station of life you will find amusements, relaxations, and enjoyments; that is, provided you be willing to make light of evils rather than

to hate them. Knowing to what sorrows we were born, there is nothing for which Nature more deserves our thanks than for having invented habit as an alleviation of misfortune, which soon accustoms us to the severest evils. No one could hold out against misfortune if it permanently exercised the same force as at its first onset. We are all chained to Fortune: some men's chain is loose and made of gold, that of others is tight and of meaner metal: but what difference does this make? we are all included in the same captivity, and even those who have bound us are bound themselves, unless you think that a chain on the left side is lighter to bear: one man may be bound by public office, another by wealth: some have to bear the weight of illustrious, some of humble birth: some are subject to the commands of others, some only to their own: some are kept in one place by being banished thither, others by being elected to the priesthood. All life is slavery: let each man therefore reconcile himself to his lot, complain of it as little as possible, and lay hold of whatever good lies within his reach. No condition can be so wretched that an impartial mind can find no compensations in it. Small sites, if ingeniously divided, may be made use of for many different purposes, and arrangement will render ever so narrow a room habitable. Call good sense to your aid against difficulties: it is possible to soften what is harsh, to widen what is too narrow, and to make heavy burdens press less severely upon one who bears them skilfully. Moreover, we ought not to allow our desires to wander far afield, but we must make them confine themselves to our immediate neighbourhood, since they will not endure to be altogether locked up. We must leave alone things which either cannot come to pass or can only be effected with difficulty, and follow after such things as are near at hand and within reach of our hopes, always remembering that all things are equally unimportant, and that though they have a different outward appearance, they are all alike empty within. Neither let us envy those who are in high places: the heights which look lofty to us are steep and rugged. Again, those whom unkind fate has placed in critical situations will be safer if they show as little pride in their proud position as may be, and do all they are able to bring down their fortunes to the level of other men's. There are many who must needs cling to their high pinnacle of power, because they cannot descend from it save by falling headlong: yet they assure us that their greatest burden is being obliged to be burdensome to others, and that they are nailed to their lofty post rather than raised to it: let them then, by dispensing justice, clemency, and kindness with an open and liberal hand, provide themselves with assistance to break their fall, and looking forward to this maintain their position more hopefully. Yet nothing sets us free from these alternations of hope and fear so well as always fixing some limit to our successes, and not allowing Fortune to choose when to stop our career, but to halt of our own accord long before we apparently need do so. By acting thus, certain desires will rouse up our spirits, and yet being confined within bounds will not lead us to embark on vast and vague enterprises.

11. These remarks of mine apply only to imperfect, commonplace, and unsound natures, not to the wise man, who needs not to walk with timid and cautious gait: for he has such confidence in himself that he does not hesitate to go directly in the teeth of Fortune, and never will give way to her. Nor indeed has he any reason for fearing her, for he counts not only chattels, property, and high office, but even his body, his eyes, his hands, and everything whose use makes life dearer to us, nay, even his very self, to be things whose possession is uncertain; he lives as though he had borrowed them, and is ready to return them cheerfully whenever they are claimed. Yet he does not hold himself cheap, because he knows that he is not his own, but performs all his duties as carefully and prudently as a pious and scrupulous man would take care of property left in his charge as trustee. When he is bidden to give them up, he will not complain of Fortune, but will say, "I

thank you for what I have had possession of: I have managed your property so as largely to increase it, but since you order me, I give it back to you and return it willingly and thankfully. If you still wish me to own anything of yours, I will keep it for you: if you have other views, I restore into your hands and make restitution of all my wrought and coined silver, my house and my household. Should Nature recall what she previously entrusted us with, let us say to her also: 'Take back my spirit, which is better than when you gave it me: I do not shuffle or hang back. Of my own free will I am ready to return what you gave me before I could think: take me away.'" What hardship can there be in returning to the place from whence one came? a man cannot live well if he knows not how to die well. We must, therefore, take away from this commodity its original value, and count the breath of life as a cheap matter. "We dislike gladiators," says Cicero, "if they are eager to save their lives by any means whatever: but we look favourably upon them if they are openly reckless of them." You may be sure that the same thing occurs with us: we often die because we are afraid of death. Fortune, which regards our lives as a show in the arena for her own enjoyment, says, "Why should I spare you, base and cowardly creature that you are? you will be pierced and hacked with all the more wounds because you know not how to offer your throat to the knife: whereas you, who receive the stroke without drawing away your neck or putting up your hands to stop it, shall both live longer and die more quickly." He who fears death will never act as becomes a living man: but he who knows that this fate was laid upon him as soon as he was conceived will live according to it, and by this strength of mind will gain this further advantage, that nothing can befall him unexpectedly: for by looking forward to everything which can happen as though it would happen to him, he takes the sting out of all evils, which can make no difference to those who expect it and are prepared to meet it: evil only comes hard upon those who have lived without giving it a thought and whose attention has been exclusively directed to happiness. Disease, captivity, disaster, conflagration, are none of them unexpected: I always knew with what disorderly company Nature had associated me. The dead have often been wailed for in my neighbourhood: the torch and taper have often been borne past my door before the bier of one who has died before his time: the crash of falling buildings has often resounded by my side: night has snatched away many of those with whom I have become intimate in the Forum, the Senate house, and in society, and has sundered the hands which were joined in friendship: ought I to be surprised if the dangers which have always been circling around me at last assail me? How large a part of mankind never thinks of storms when about to set sail? I shall never be ashamed to quote a good saying because it comes from a bad author. Publilius, who was a more powerful writer than any of our other playwrights, whether comic or tragic, whenever he chose to rise above farcical absurdities and speeches addressed to the gallery, among many other verses too noble even for tragedy, let alone for comedy, has this one:—

What one hath suffered may befall us all.

If a man takes this into his inmost heart and looks upon all the misfortunes of other men, of which there is always a great plenty, in this spirit, remembering that there is nothing to prevent their coming upon him also, he will arm himself against them long before they attack him. It is too late to school the mind to endurance of peril after peril has come. "I did not think this would happen," and "Would you ever have believed that this would have happened?" say you. But why should it not? Where are the riches after which want, hunger, and beggary do not follow? what office is there whose purple robe, augur's staff, and patrician reins have not as their accompaniment rags and banishment, the brand of infamy, a thousand disgraces, and utter reprobation? what kingdom is there for which ruin, trampling under foot, a tyrant and a butcher are not ready at hand? nor are these matters divided by long periods of time, but there is but the space of an hour between sitting on the throne ourselves and clasping the knees of someone else as suppliants. Know then that every station of life is transitory, and that what has ever happened to anybody may happen to you also. You are wealthy: are you wealthier than Pompeius? Yet when Gaius, his old relative and new host, opened Caesar's house to him in order that he might close his own, he lacked both bread and water: though he owned so many rivers which both rose and discharged themselves within his dominions, yet he had to beg for drops of water: he perished of hunger and thirst in the palace of his relative, while his heir was contracting for a public funeral for one who was in want of food. You have filled public offices: were they either as important, as unlooked-for, or as all-embracing as those of Sejanus? Yet on the day on which the Senate disgraced him, the people tore him to pieces: the executioner could find no part left large enough to drag to the Tiber, of one upon whom gods and men had showered all that could be given to man. You are a king: I will not bid you go to Croesus for an example, he who while yet alive saw his funeral pile both lighted and extinguished, being made to outlive not only his kingdom but even his own death, nor to Jugurtha, whom the people of Rome beheld as a captive within the year in which they had feared him. We have seen Ptolemaeus King of Africa, and Mithridates King of Armenia, under the charge of Gaius's guards: the former was sent into exile, the latter chose it in order to make his exile more honourable. Among such continual topsy-turvy changes, unless you expect that whatever can happen will happen to you, you give adversity power against you, a power which can be destroyed by any one who looks at it beforehand.

12. The next point to these will be to take care that we do not labour for what is vain, or labour in vain: that is to say,

neither to desire what we are not able to obtain, nor yet, having obtained our desire too late, and after much toil to discover the folly of our wishes: in other words, that our labour may not be without result, and that the result may not be unworthy of our labour: for as a rule sadness arises from one of these two things, either from want of success or from being ashamed of having succeeded. We must limit the running to and fro which most men practise, rambling about houses, theatres, and market-places. They mind other men's business, and always seem as though they themselves had something to do. If you ask one of them as he comes out of his own door, "Whither are you going?" he will answer, "By Hercules, I do not know: but I shall see some people and do something." They wander purposelessly seeking for something to do, and do, not what they have made up their minds to do, but what has casually fallen in their way. They move uselessly and without any plan, just like ants crawling over bushes, which creep up to the top and then down to the bottom again without gaining anything. Many men spend their lives in exactly the same fashion, which one may call a state of restless indolence. You would pity some of them when you see them running as if their house was on fire: they actually jostle all whom they meet, and hurry along themselves and others with them, though all the while they are going to salute someone who will not return their greeting, or to attend the funeral of someone whom they did not know: they are going to hear the verdict on one who often goes to law, or to see the wedding of one who often gets married: they will follow a man's litter, and in some places will even carry it: afterwards returning home weary with idleness, they swear that they themselves do not know why they went out, or where they have been, and on the following day they will wander through the same round again. Let all your work, therefore, have some purpose, and keep some object in view: these restless people are not made restless by labour, but are driven out of their minds by mistaken ideas: for even they do not put themselves in motion without any hope: they are excited by the outward appearance of something, and their crazy mind cannot see its futility. In the same way every one of those who walk out to swell the crowd in the streets, is led round the city by worthless and empty reasons; the dawn drives him forth, although he has nothing to do, and after he has pushed his way into many men's doors, and saluted their nomenclators one after the other, and been turned away from many others, he finds that the most difficult person of all to find at home is himself. From this evil habit comes that worst of all vices, talebearing and prying into public and private secrets, and the knowledge of many things which it is neither safe to tell nor safe to listen to.

13. It was, I imagine, following out this principle that Democritus taught that "he who would live at peace must not do much business either public or private," referring of course to unnecessary business: for if there be any necessity for it we ought to transact not only much but endless business, both public and private; in cases, however, where no solemn duty invites us to act, we had better keep ourselves quiet: for he who does many things often puts himself in Fortune's power, and it is safest not to tempt her often, but always to remember her existence, and never to promise oneself anything on her security. I will set sail unless anything happens to prevent me, I shall be praetor, if nothing hinders me, my financial operations will succeed, unless anything goes wrong with them. This is why we say that nothing befalls the wise man which he did not expect—we do not make him exempt from the chances of human life, but from its mistakes, nor does everything happen to him as he wished it would, but as he thought it would: now his first thought was that his purpose might meet with some resistance, and the pain of disappointed wishes must affect a man's mind less severely if he has not been at all events confident of success.

14. Moreover, we ought to cultivate an easy temper, and not become overfond of the lot which fate has assigned to us, but transfer ourselves to whatever other condition chance may lead us to, and fear no alteration, either in our purposes or our position in life, provided that we do not become subject to caprice, which of all vices is the most hostile to repose: for obstinacy, from which Fortune often wrings some concession, must needs be anxious and unhappy, but caprice, which can never restrain itself, must be more so. Both of these qualities, both that of altering nothing, and that of being dissatisfied with everything, are enemies to repose. The mind ought in all cases to be called away from the contemplation of external things to that of itself: let it confide in itself, rejoice in itself, admire its own works; avoid as far as may be those of others, and devote itself to itself; let it not feel losses, and put a good construction even upon misfortunes. Zeno, the chief of our school, when he heard the news of a shipwreck, in which all his property had been lost, remarked, "Fortune bids me follow philosophy in lighter marching order." A tyrant threatened Theodorus with death, and even with want of burial. "You are able to please yourself," he answered, "my half pint of blood is in your power: for, as for burial, what a fool you must be if you suppose that I care whether I rot above ground or under it." Julius Kanus, a man of peculiar greatness, whom even the fact of his having been born in this century does not prevent our admiring, had a long dispute with Gaius, and when as he was going away that Phalaris of a man said to him, "That you may not delude yourself with any foolish hopes, I have ordered you to be executed," he answered, "I thank you, most excellent prince." I am not sure what he meant: for many ways of explaining his conduct occur to me. Did he wish to be reproachful, and to show him how great his cruelty must be if death became a kindness? or did he upbraid him with his accustomed insanity? for even those whose children were put to death, and whose goods were confiscated, used to thank him: or was it that he willingly received death,

regarding it as freedom? Whatever he meant, it was a magnanimous answer. Someone may say, "After this Gaius might
have let him live." Kanus had no fear of this: the good faith
with which Gaius carried out such orders as these was well
known. Will you believe that he passed the ten intervening
days before his execution without the slightest despondency?
it is marvellous how that man spoke and acted, and how
peaceful he was. He was playing at draughts when the centurion in charge of a number of those who were going to be
executed bade him join them: on the summons he counted
his men and said to his companion, "Mind you do not tell a
lie after my death, and say that you won"; then, turning to the
centurion, he said "You will bear me witness that I am one
man ahead of him." Do you think that Kanus played upon
that draught-board? nay, he played with it. His friends were
sad at being about to lose so great a man: "Why," asked he,
"are you sorrowful? you are enquiring whether our souls are
immortal, but I shall presently know." Nor did he up to the
very end cease his search after truth, and raised arguments
upon the subject of his own death. His own teacher of philosophy accompanied him, and they were not far from the hill
on which the daily sacrifice to Caesar our god was offered,
when he said, "What are you thinking of now, Kanus? or
what are your ideas?" "I have decided," answered Kanus, "at
that most swiftly passing moment of all to watch whether
the spirit will be conscious of the act of leaving the body."
He promised, too, that if he made any discoveries, he would
come round to his friends and tell them what the condition
of the souls of the departed might be. Here was peace in the
very midst of the storm: here was a soul worthy of eternal life,
which used its own fate as a proof of truth, which when at the
last step of life experimented upon his fleeting breath, and
did not merely continue to learn until he died, but learned
something even from death itself. No man has carried the
life of a philosopher further. I will not hastily leave the subject of a great man, and one who deserves to be spoken of

with respect: I will hand thee down to all posterity, thou most noble heart, chief among the many victims of Gaius.

15. Yet we gain nothing by getting rid of all personal causes of sadness, for sometimes we are possessed by hatred of the human race. When you reflect how rare simplicity is, how unknown innocence, how seldom faith is kept, unless it be to our advantage, when you remember such numbers of successful crimes, so many equally hateful losses and gains of lust, and ambition so impatient even of its own natural limits that it is willing to purchase distinction by baseness, the mind seems as it were cast into darkness, and shadows rise before it as though the virtues were all overthrown and we were no longer allowed to hope to possess them or benefited by their possession. We ought therefore to bring ourselves into such a state of mind that all the vices of the vulgar may not appear hateful to us, but merely ridiculous, and we should imitate Democritus rather than Heraclitus. The latter of these, whenever he appeared in public, used to weep, the former to laugh: the one thought all human doings to be follies, the other thought them to be miseries. We must take a higher view of all things, and bear with them more easily: it better becomes a man to scoff at life than to lament over it. Add to this that he who laughs at the human race deserves better of it than he who mourns for it, for the former leaves it some good hopes of improvement, while the latter stupidly weeps over what he has given up all hopes of mending. He who after surveying the universe cannot control his laughter shows, too, a greater mind than he who cannot restrain his tears, because his mind is only affected in the slightest possible degree, and he does not think that any part of all this apparatus is either important, or serious, or unhappy. As for the several causes which render us happy or sorrowful, let everyone describe them for himself, and learn the truth of Bion's saying, "That all the doings of men were very like what he began with, and that there is nothing in their lives

which is more holy or decent than their conception." Yet it is better to accept public morals and human vices calmly without bursting into either laughter or tears; for to be hurt by the sufferings of others is to be forever miserable, while to enjoy the sufferings of others is an inhuman pleasure, just as it is a useless piece of humanity to weep and pull a long face because someone is burying his son. In one's own misfortunes, also, one ought so to conduct oneself as to bestow upon them just as much sorrow as reason, not as much as custom requires: for many shed tears in order to show them, and whenever no one is looking at them their eyes are dry, but they think it disgraceful not to weep when everyone does so. So deeply has this evil of being guided by the opinion of others taken root in us, that even grief, the simplest of all emotions, begins to be counterfeited.

16. There comes now a part of our subject which is wont with good cause to make one sad and anxious: I mean when good men come to bad ends; when Socrates is forced to die in prison, Rutilius to live in exile, Pompeius and Cicero to offer their necks to the swords of their own followers, when the great Cato, that living image of virtue, falls upon his sword and rips up both himself and the republic, one cannot help being grieved that Fortune should bestow her gifts so unjustly: what, too, can a good man hope to obtain when he sees the best of men meeting with the worst fates. Well, but see how each of them endured his fate, and if they endured it bravely, long in your heart for courage as great as theirs; if they died in a womanish and cowardly manner, nothing was lost: either they deserved that you should admire their courage, or else they did not deserve that you should wish to imitate their cowardice: for what can be more shameful than that the greatest men should die so bravely as to make people cowards. Let us praise one who deserves such constant praises, and say, "The braver you are, the happier you are! You have escaped from all accidents, jealousies, diseases:

you have escaped from prison: the gods have not thought
you worthy of ill-fortune, but have thought that fortune no
longer deserved to have any power over you": but when anyone shrinks back in the hour of death and looks longingly
at life, we must lay hands upon him. I will never weep for a
man who dies cheerfully, nor for one who dies weeping: the
former wipes away my tears, the latter by his tears makes himself unworthy that any should be shed for him. Shall I weep
for Hercules because he was burned alive, or for Regulus
because he was pierced by so many nails, or for Cato because
he tore open his wounds a second time? All these men discovered how at the cost of a small portion of time they might
obtain immortality, and by their deaths gained eternal life.

17. It also proves a fertile source of troubles if you take pains
to conceal your feelings and never show yourself to anyone
undisguised, but, as many men do, live an artificial life, in
order to impose upon others: for the constant watching of
himself becomes a torment to a man, and he dreads being
caught doing something at variance with his usual habits,
and, indeed, we never can be at our ease if we imagine that
everyone who looks at us is weighing our real value: for many
things occur which strip people of their disguise, however
reluctantly they may part with it, and even if all this trouble
about oneself is successful, still life is neither happy nor safe
when one always has to wear a mask. But what pleasure is there
in that honest straight-forwardness which is its own ornament, and which conceals no part of its character? Yet even
this life, which hides nothing from any one runs some risk
of being despised; for there are people who disdain whatever
they come close to: but there is no danger of virtue's becoming contemptible when she is brought near our eyes, and it
is better to be scorned for one's simplicity than to bear the
burden of unceasing hypocrisy. Still, we must observe moderation in this matter, for there is a great difference between
living simply and living slovenly. Moreover, we ought to retire

a great deal into ourselves: for association with persons unlike ourselves upsets all that we had arranged, rouses the passions which were at rest, and rubs into a sore any weak or imperfectly healed place in our minds. Nevertheless we ought to mix up these two things, and to pass our lives alternately in solitude and among throngs of people; for the former will make us long for the society of mankind, the latter for that of ourselves, and the one will counteract the other: solitude will cure us when we are sick of crowds, and crowds will cure us when we are sick of solitude. Neither ought we always to keep the mind strained to the same pitch, but it ought sometimes to be relaxed by amusement. Socrates did not blush to play with little boys, Cato used to refresh his mind with wine after he had wearied it with application to affairs of state, and Scipio would move his triumphal and soldierly limbs to the sound of music, not with a feeble and halting gait, as is the fashion nowadays, when we sway in our very walk with more than womanly weakness, but dancing as men were wont in the days of old on sportive and festal occasions, with manly bounds, thinking it no harm to be seen so doing even by their enemies. Men's minds ought to have relaxation: they rise up better and more vigorous after rest. We must not force crops from rich fields, for an unbroken course of heavy crops will soon exhaust their fertility, and so also the liveliness of our minds will be destroyed by unceasing labour, but they will recover their strength after a short period of rest and relief: for continuous toil produces a sort of numbness and sluggishness. Men would not be so eager for this, if play and amusement did not possess natural attractions for them, although constant indulgence in them takes away all gravity and all strength from the mind: for sleep, also, is necessary for our refreshment, yet if you prolong it for days and nights together it will become death. There is a great difference between slackening your hold of a thing and letting it go. The founders of our laws appointed festivals, in order that men might be publicly encouraged to be cheerful, and they thought it necessary to vary our labours with amusements, and, as I said before, some great men have been wont to give themselves a certain number of holidays in every month, and some divided every day into play-time and work-time. Thus, I remember that great orator Asinius Pollio would not attend to any business after the tenth hour: he would not even read letters after that time for fear some new trouble should arise, but in those two hours used to get rid of the weariness which he had contracted during the whole day. Some rest in the middle of the day, and reserve some light occupation for the afternoon. Our ancestors, too, forbade any new motion to be made in the Senate after the tenth hour. Soldiers divide their watches, and those who have just returned from active service are allowed to sleep the whole night undisturbed. We must humour our minds and grant them rest from time to time, which acts upon them like food, and restores their strength. It does good also to take walks out of doors, that our spirits may be raised and refreshed by the open air and fresh breeze: sometimes we gain strength by driving in a carriage, by travel, by change of air, or by social meals and a more generous allowance of wine: at times we ought to drink even to intoxication, not so as to drown, but merely to dip ourselves in wine: for wine washes away troubles and dislodges them from the depths of the mind, and acts as a remedy to sorrow as it does to some diseases. The inventor of wine is called Liber, not from the licence which he gives to our tongues, but because he liberates the mind from the bondage of cares, and emancipates it, animates it, and renders it more daring in all that it attempts. Yet moderation is wholesome both in freedom and in wine. It is believed that Solon and Arcesilaus used to drink deep. Cato is reproached with drunkenness: but whoever casts this in his teeth will find it easier to turn his reproach into a commendation than to prove that Cato did anything wrong: however, we ought not to do it often, for fear the mind should contract evil habits, though it ought sometimes to be forced into frolic and frankness, and to cast off dull sobriety for a while. If we believe the Greek poet, "it is sometimes pleasant to be mad"; again, Plato always knocked in vain at the door of poetry when he was sober; or, if we trust Aristotle, no great genius has ever been without a touch of insanity. The mind cannot use lofty language, above that of the common herd, unless it be excited. When it has spurned aside the commonplace environments of custom, and rises sublime, instinct with sacred fire, then alone can it chant a song too grand for mortal lips: as long as it continues to dwell within itself it cannot rise to any pitch of splendour: it must break away from the beaten track, and lash itself to frenzy, till it gnaws the curb and rushes away bearing up its rider to heights whither it would fear to climb when alone.

I have now, my beloved Serenus, given you an account of what things can preserve peace of mind, what things can restore it to us, what can arrest the vices which secretly undermine it: yet be assured that none of these is strong enough to enable us to retain so fleeting a blessing, unless we watch over our vacillating mind with intense and unremitting care.

ON CLEMENCY

ADDRESSED TO NERO CAESAR

Part I

1. I have determined to write a book upon clemency, Nero Caesar,
    in order that I may as it were serve as a mirror to you, and let
    you see yourself arriving at the greatest of all pleasures. For
    although the true enjoyment of good deeds consists in the
    performance of them, and virtues have no adequate reward
    beyond themselves, still it is worth your while to consider
    and investigate a good conscience from every point of view,
    and afterwards to cast your eyes upon this enormous mass
    of mankind—quarrelsome, factious, and passionate as they
    are; likely, if they could throw off the yoke of your govern-
    ment, to take pleasure alike in the ruin of themselves and of
    one another—and thus to commune with yourself:—"Have I
    of all mankind been chosen and thought fit to perform the
    office of a god upon earth? I am the arbiter of life and death
    to mankind: it rests with me to decide what lot and position
    in life each man possesses: fortune makes use of my mouth to
    announce what she bestows on each man: cities and nations
    are moved to joy by my words: no region anywhere can flour-
    ish without my favour and good will: all these thousands of
    swords now restrained by my authority, would be drawn at
    a sign from me: it rests with me to decide which tribes shall

be utterly exterminated, which shall be moved into other lands, which shall receive and which shall be deprived of liberty, what kings shall be reduced to slavery and whose heads shall be crowned, what cities shall be destroyed and what new ones shall be founded. In this position of enormous power I am not tempted to punish men unjustly by anger, by youthful impulse, by the recklessness and insolence of men, which often overcomes the patience even of the best regulated minds, not even that terrible vanity, so common among great sovereigns, of displaying my power by inspiring terror. My sword is sheathed, nay, fixed in its sheath: I am sparing of the blood even of the lowest of my subjects: a man who has nothing else to recommend him, will nevertheless find favour in my eyes because he is a man. I keep harshness concealed, but I have clemency always at hand: I watch myself as carefully as though I had to give an account of my actions to those laws which I have brought out of darkness and neglect into the light of day. I have been moved to compassion by the youth of one culprit, and the age of another: I have spared one man because of his great place, another on account of his insignificance: when I could find no reason for showing mercy, I have had mercy upon myself. I am prepared this day, should the gods demand it, to render to them an account of the human race." You, Caesar, can boldly say that everything which has come into your charge has been kept safe, and that the state has neither openly nor secretly suffered any loss at your hands. You have coveted a glory which is most rare, and which has been obtained by no emperor before you, that of innocence. Your remarkable goodness is not thrown away, nor is it ungratefully or spitefully undervalued. Men feel gratitude towards you: no one person ever was so dear to another as you are to the people of Rome, whose great and enduring benefit you are. You have, however, taken upon yourself a mighty burden: no one any longer speaks of the good times of the late Emperor Augustus, or the first years of the reign of Tiberius, or proposes for your imitation any model outside yourself: yours is a pattern reign. This would have been difficult had your goodness of heart not been innate, but merely adopted for a time; for no one can wear a mask for long, and fictitious qualities soon give place to true ones. Those which are founded upon truth, and which, so to speak, grow out of a solid basis, only become greater and better as time goes on. The Roman people were in a state of great hazard as long as it was uncertain how your generous disposition would turn out; now, however, the prayers of the community are sure of an answer, for there is no fear that you should suddenly forget your own character. Indeed, excess of happiness makes men greedy, and our desires are never so moderate as to be bounded by what they have obtained: great successes become the stepping-stones to greater ones, and those who have obtained more than they hoped, entertain even more extravagant hopes than before; yet by all your countrymen we hear it admitted that they are now happy, and moreover, that nothing can be added to the blessings that they enjoy, except that they should be eternal. Many circumstances force this admission from them, although it is the one which men are least willing to make: we enjoy a profound and prosperous peace, the power of the law has been openly asserted in the sight of all men, and raised beyond the reach of any violent interference: the form of our government is so happy, as to contain all the essentials of liberty except the power of destroying itself. It is nevertheless your clemency which is most especially admired by the high and low alike: every man enjoys or hopes to enjoy the other blessings of your rule according to the measure of his own personal good fortune, whereas from your clemency all hope alike: no one has so much confidence in his own innocence, as not to feel glad that in your presence stands a clemency which is ready to make allowance for human errors.

2.   I know, however, that there are some who imagine that clemency only saves the life of every villain, because clemency is

useless except after conviction, and alone of all the virtues has no function among the innocent. But in the first place, although a physician is only useful to the sick, yet he is held in honour among the healthy also; and so clemency, though she be invoked by those who deserve punishment, is respected by innocent people as well. Next, she can exist also in the person of the innocent, because sometimes misfortune takes the place of crime; indeed, clemency not only succours the innocent, but often the virtuous, since in the course of time it happens that men are punished for actions which deserve praise. Besides this, there is a large part of mankind which might return to virtue if the hope of pardon were not denied them. Yet it is not right to pardon indiscriminately; for when no distinction is made between good and bad men, disorder follows, and all vices break forth; we must therefore take care to distinguish those characters which admit of reform from those which are hopelessly depraved. Neither ought we to show an indiscriminate and general, nor yet an exclusive clemency; for to pardon every one is as great cruelty as to pardon none; we must take a middle course; but as it is difficult to find the true mean, let us be careful, if we depart from it, to do so upon the side of humanity.

3. But these matters will be treated of better in their own place. I will now divide this whole subject into three parts. The first will be of gentleness of temper: the second will be that which explains the nature and disposition of clemency; for since there are certain vices which have the semblance of virtue, they cannot be separated unless you stamp upon them the marks which distinguish them from one another: in the third place we shall inquire how the mind may be led to practise this virtue, how it may strengthen it, and by habit make it its own.

That clemency, which is the most humane of virtues, is that which best befits a man, is necessarily an axiom, not only among our own sect, which regards man as a social animal, born for the good of the whole community, but even among those philosophers who give him up entirely to pleasure, and whose words and actions have no other aim than their own personal advantage. If man, as they argue, seeks for quiet and repose, what virtue is there which is more agreeable to his nature than clemency, which loves peace and restrains him from violence? Now clemency becomes no one more than a king or a prince; for great power is glorious and admirable only when it is beneficent; since to be powerful only for mischief is the power of a pestilence. That man's greatness alone rests upon a secure foundation, whom all men know to be as much on their side as he is above them, of whose watchful care for the safety of each and all of them they receive daily proofs, at whose approach they do not fly in terror, as though some evil and dangerous animal had sprung out from its den, but flock to him as they would to the bright and health-giving sunshine. They are perfectly ready to fling themselves upon the swords of conspirators in his defence, to offer their bodies if his only path to safety must be formed of corpses: they protect his sleep by nightly watches, they surround him and defend him on every side, and expose themselves to the dangers which menace him. It is not without good reason that nations and cities thus agree in sacrificing their lives and property for the defence and the love of their king whenever their leader's safety demands it; men do not hold themselves cheap, nor are they insane when so many thousands are put to the sword for the sake of one man, and when by so many deaths they save the life of one man alone, who not unfrequently is old and feeble. Just as the entire body is commanded by the mind, and although the body be so much larger and more beautiful while the mind is impalpable and hidden, and we are not certain as to where it is concealed, yet the hands, feet, and eyes work for it, the skin protects it; at its bidding we either lie still or move restlessly about; when it gives the word, if it be an avaricious master, we scour the sea in search of gain, or if it be ambitious we straightaway place our right hand in the flames like Mucius, or leap into the pit like Curtius, so likewise this enormous multitude which surrounds one man is directed by his will, is guided by his intellect, and would break and hurl itself into ruin by its own strength, if it were not upheld by his wisdom.

4. Men therefore love their own safety, when they draw up vast legions in battle on behalf of one man, when they rush to the front, and expose their breasts to wounds, for fear that their leader's standards should be driven back. He is the bond which fastens the commonwealth together, he is the breath of life to all those thousands, who by themselves would become merely an encumbrance and a source of plunder if that directing mind were withdrawn:—

> Bees have but one mind, till their king doth die,
> But when he dies, disorderly they fly.

Such a misfortune will be the end of the peace of Rome, it will wreck the prosperity of this great people; the nation will be free from this danger as long as it knows how to endure the reins: should it ever break them, or refuse to have them replaced if they were to fall off by accident, then this mighty whole, this complex fabric of government will fly asunder into many fragments, and the last day of Rome's empire will be that upon which it forgets how to obey. For this reason we need not wonder that princes, kings, and all other protectors of a state, whatever their titles may be, should be loved beyond the circle of their immediate relatives; for since right-thinking men prefer the interests of the state to their own, it follows that he who bears the burden of state affairs must be dearer to them than their own friends. Indeed, the emperor long ago identified himself so thoroughly with the state, that neither of them could be separated without injury to both, because the one requires power, while the other requires a head.

5. My argument seems to have wandered somewhat far from the subject, but, by Hercules, it really is very much to the point. For if, as we may infer from what has been said, you are the soul of the state, and the state is your body, you will perceive, I imagine, how necessary clemency is; for when you appear to spare another, you are really sparing yourself. You ought therefore to spare even blameworthy citizens, just as you spare weakly limbs; and when blood-letting becomes necessary, you must hold your hand, lest you should cut deeper than you need. Clemency therefore, as I said before, naturally befits all mankind, but more especially rulers, because in their case there is more for it to save, and it is displayed upon a greater scale. Cruelty in a private man can do but very little harm; but the ferocity of princes is war. Although there is a harmony between all the virtues, and no one is better or more honourable than another, yet some virtues befit some persons better than others. Magnanimity befits all mortal men, even the humblest of all; for what can be greater or braver than to resist ill fortune? Yet this virtue of magnanimity occupies a wider room in prosperity, and shows to greater advantage on the judgment seat than on the floor of the court. On the other hand, clemency renders every house into which it is admitted happy and peaceful; but though it is more rare, it is on that account even more admirable in a palace. What can be more remarkable than that he whose anger might be indulged without fear of the consequences, whose decision, even though a harsh one, would be approved even by those who were to suffer by it, whom no one can interrupt, and of whom indeed, should he become violently enraged, no one would dare to beg for mercy, should apply a check to himself and use his power in a better and calmer spirit, reflecting: "Anyone may break the law to kill a man, no one but I can break it to save him"? A great position requires a great mind, for unless the mind raises itself to and even above the level of its station, it will degrade its station and draw it down to the earth; now it is the property of a great mind to

be calm and tranquil and to look down upon outrages and insults with contempt. It is a womanish thing to rage with passion; it is the part of wild beasts, and that, too, not of the most noble ones, to bite and worry the fallen. Elephants and lions pass by those whom they have struck down; inveteracy is the quality of ignoble animals. Fierce and implacable rage does not befit a king, because he does not preserve his superiority over the man to whose level he descends by indulging in rage; but if he grants their lives and honours to those who are in jeopardy and who deserve to lose them, he does what can only be done by an absolute ruler; for life may be torn away even from those who are above us in station, but can never be granted save to those who are below us. To save men's lives is the privilege of the loftiest station, which never deserves admiration so much as when it is able to act like the gods, by whose kindness good and bad men alike are brought into the world. Thus a prince, imitating the mind of a god, ought to look with pleasure on some of his countrymen because they are useful and good men, while he ought to allow others to remain to fill up the roll; he ought to be pleased with the existence of the former, and to endure that of the latter.

6. Look at this city of Rome, in which the widest streets become choked whenever anything stops the crowds which unceasingly pour through them like raging torrents, in which the people streaming to three theatres demand the roads at the same time, in which the produce of the entire world is consumed, and reflect what a desolate waste it would become if only those were left in it whom a strict judge would acquit. How few magistrates are there who ought not to be condemned by the very same laws which they administer? How few prosecutors are themselves faultless? I imagine, also, that few men are less willing to grant pardon, than those who have often had to beg it for themselves. We have all of us sinned, some more deeply than others, some of set purpose,

some either by chance impulse or led away by the wickedness of others; some of us have not stood bravely enough by our good resolutions, and have lost our innocence, although unwillingly and after a struggle; nor have we only sinned, but to the very end of our lives we shall continue to sin. Even if there be anyone who has so thoroughly cleansed his mind that nothing can hereafter throw him into disorder or deceive him, yet even he has reached this state of innocence through sin.

7. Since I have made mention of the gods, I shall state the best model on which a prince may mould his life to be, that he deal with his countrymen as he would that the gods may deal with himself. Is it then desirable that the gods should show no mercy upon sins and mistakes, and that they should harshly pursue us to our ruin? In that case what king will be safe? Whose limbs will not be torn asunder and collected by the soothsayers? If, on the other hand, the gods are placable and kind, and do not at once avenge the crimes of the powerful with thunderbolts, is it not far more just that a man set in authority over other men should exercise his power in a spirit of clemency and should consider whether the condition of the world is more beauteous and pleasant to the eyes on a fine calm day, or when everything is shaken with frequent thunderclaps and when lightning flashes on all sides! Yet the appearance of a peaceful and constitutional reign is the same as that of the calm and brilliant sky. A cruel reign is disordered and hidden in darkness, and while all shake with terror at the sudden explosions, not even he who caused all this disturbance escapes unharmed. It is easier to find excuses for private men who obstinately claim their rights; possibly they may have been injured, and their rage may spring from their wrongs; besides this, they fear to be despised, and not to return the injuries which they have received looks like weakness rather than clemency; but one who can easily avenge himself, if he neglects to do so, is certain to gain praise for

goodness of heart. Those who are born in a humble station may with greater freedom exercise violence, go to law, engage in quarrels, and indulge their angry passions; even blows count for little between two equals; but in the case of a king, even loud clamour and unmeasured talk are unbecoming.

8.   You think it a serious matter to take away from kings the right of free speech which the humblest enjoy. "This," you say, "is to be a subject, not a king." What, do you not find that we have the command, you the subjection? Your position is quite different to that of those who lie hid in the crowd which they never leave, whose very virtues cannot be manifested without a long struggle, and whose vices are shrouded in obscurity; rumour catches up your acts and sayings, and therefore no persons ought to be more careful of their reputation than those who are certain to have a great one, whatsoever one they may have deserved. How many things there are that you may not do which, thanks to you, we may do! I am able to walk alone without fear in any part of Rome whatever, although no companion accompanies me, though there is no guard at my house, no sword by my side. You must live armed in the peace which you maintain. You cannot stray away from your position; it besets you, and follows you with mighty pomp wherever you go. This slavery of not being able to sink one's rank belongs to the highest position of all; yet it is a burden which you share with the gods. They too are held fast in heaven, and it is no more possible for them to come down than it is safe for you; you are chained to your lofty pinnacle. Of our movements few persons are aware; we can go forth and return home and change our dress without its being publicly known; but you are no more able to hide yourself than the sun. A strong light is all around you, the eyes of all are turned towards it. Do you think you are leaving your house? nay, you are dawning upon the world. You cannot speak without all nations everywhere hearing your voice; you cannot be angry, without making everything tremble,

because you can strike no one without shaking all around him. Just as thunderbolts when they fall endanger few men but terrify all, so the chastisement inflicted by great potentates terrify more widely than they injure, and that for good reasons; for in the case of one whose power is absolute, men do not think of what he has done, so much as of what he may do. Add to this that private men endure wrongs more tamely, because they have already endured others; the safety of kings on the other hand is more surely founded on kindness, because frequent punishment may crush the hatred of a few, but excites that of all. A king ought to wish to pardon while he has still grounds for being severe; if he acts otherwise, just as lopped trees sprout forth again with numberless boughs, and many kinds of crops are cut down in order that they may grow more thickly, so a cruel king increases the number of his enemies by destroying them; for the parents and children of those who are put to death, and their relatives and friends, step into the place of each victim.

9.   I wish to prove the truth of this by an example drawn from your own family. The late Emperor Augustus was a mild prince, if in estimating his character one reckons from the era of his reign; yet he appealed to arms while the state was shared among the triumvirate. When he was just of your age, at the end of his twenty-second year, he had already hidden daggers under the clothes of his friends, he had already conspired to assassinate Marcus Antonius, the consul, he had already taken part in the proscription. But when he had passed his sixtieth year, and was staying in Gaul, intelligence was brought to him that Lucius Cinna, a dull man, was plotting against him: the plot was betrayed by one of the conspirators, who told him where, when, and in what manner Cinna meant to attack him. Augustus determined to consult his own safety against this man, and ordered a council of his own friends to be summoned. He passed a disturbed night, reflecting that he would be obliged to condemn to death a

youth of noble birth, who was guilty of no crime save this one, and who was the grandson of Gnaeus Pompeius. He, who had sat at dinner and heard M. Antonius read aloud his edict for the proscription, could not now bear to put one single man to death. With groans he kept at intervals making various inconsistent exclamations:—"What! shall I allow my assassin to walk about at his ease while I am racked by fears? Shall the man not be punished who has plotted not merely to slay but actually to sacrifice at the altar" (for the conspirators intended to attack him when he was sacrificing), "now when there is peace by land and sea, that life which so many civil wars have sought in vain, which has passed unharmed through so many battles of fleets and armies?"

Then, after an interval of silence, he would say to himself in a far louder, angrier tone than he had used to Cinna, "Why do you live, if it be to so many men's advantage that you should die? Is there no end to these executions? to this bloodshed? I am a figure set up for nobly born youths to sharpen their swords on. Is life worth having, if so many must perish to prevent my losing it?" At last his wife Livia interrupted him, saying: "Will you take a woman's advice? Do as the physicians do, who, when the usual remedies fail, try their opposites. Hitherto you have gained nothing by harsh measures: Salvidienus has been followed by Lepidus, Lepidus by Muraena, Muraena by Caepio, and Caepio by Egnatius, not to mention others of whom one feels ashamed of their having dared to attempt so great a deed. Now try what effect clemency will have: pardon Lucius Cinna. He has been detected, he cannot now do you any harm, and he can do your reputation much good." Delighted at finding someone to support his own view of the case, he thanked his wife, straightaway ordered his friends, whose counsel he had asked for, to be told that he did not require their advice, and summoned Cinna alone. After ordering a second seat to be placed for Cinna, he sent everyone else out of the room, and said:— "The first request which I have to make of you is, that you will

not interrupt me while I am speaking to you: that you will
not cry out in the middle of my address to you: you shall be
allowed time to speak freely in answer to me. Cinna, when I
found you in the enemy's camp, you who had not become but
were actually born my enemy, I saved your life, and restored
to you the whole of your father's estate. You are now so prosperous and so rich, that many of the victorious party envy
you, the vanquished one: when you were a candidate for the
priesthood I passed over many others whose parents had
served with me in the wars, and gave it to you: and now, after
I have deserved so well of you, you have made up your mind
to kill me." When at this word the man exclaimed that he
was far from being so insane, Augustus replied, "You do not
keep your promise, Cinna; it was agreed upon between us
that you should not interrupt me. I repeat, you are preparing
to kill me." He then proceeded to tell him of the place, the
names of his accomplices, the day, the way in which they had
arranged to do the deed, and which of them was to give the
fatal stab. When he saw Cinna's eyes fixed upon the ground,
and that he was silent, no longer because of the agree-
ment, but from consciousness of his guilt, he said, "What is
your intention in doing this? is it that you yourself may be
emperor? The Roman people must indeed be in a bad way if
nothing but my life prevents your ruling over them. You cannot even maintain the dignity of your own house: you have
recently been defeated in a legal encounter by the superior
influence of a freedman: and so you can find no easier task
than to call your friends to rally round you against Caesar.
Come, now, if you think that I alone stand in the way of your
ambition; will Paulus and Fabius Maximus, will the Cossi
and the Servilii and all that band of nobles, whose names
are no empty pretence, but whose ancestry really renders
them illustrious—will they endure that you should rule over
them?" Not to fill up the greater part of this book by repeat-
ing the whole of his speech—for he is known to have spoken
for more than two hours, lengthening out this punishment,

which was the only one which he intended to inflict—he said at last: "Cinna, I grant you your life for the second time: when I gave it you before you were an open enemy, you are now a secret plotter and parricide. From this day forth let us be friends: let us try which of us is the more sincere, I in giving you your life, or you in owing your life to me." After this he of his own accord bestowed the consulship upon him, complaining of his not venturing to offer himself as a candidate for that office, and found him ever afterwards his most grateful and loyal adherent. Cinna made the emperor his sole heir, and no one ever again formed any plot against him.

10. Your great-great-grandfather spared the vanquished: for whom could he have ruled over, had he not spared them? He recruited Sallustius, the Cocoeii, the Deillii, and the whole inner circle of his court from the camp of his opponents. Soon afterwards his clemency gave him a Domitius, a Messala, an Asinius, a Cicero, and all the flower of the state. For what a long time he waited for Lepidus to die: for years he allowed him to retain all the insignia of royalty, and did not allow the office of pontifex maximus to be conferred upon himself until after Lepidus's death; for he wished it to be called an honourable office rather than a spoil stripped from a vanquished foe. It was this clemency which made him end his days in safety and security: this it was which rendered him popular and beloved, although he had laid his hands on the neck of the Romans when they were still unused to bearing the yoke: this gives him even at the present day a reputation such as hardly any prince has enjoyed during his own lifetime. We believe him to be a god, and not merely because we are bidden to do so. We declare that Augustus was a good emperor, and that he was well worthy to bear his parent's name, for no other reason than because he did not even show cruelty in avenging personal insults, which most princes feel more keenly than actual injuries; because he smiled at scandalous jests against himself, because it was evident that he

himself suffered when he punished others, because he was so far from putting to death even those whom he had convicted of intriguing with his daughter, that when they were banished he gave them passports to enable them to travel more safely. When you know that there will be many who will take your quarrel upon themselves, and will try to gain your favour by the murder of your enemies, you do indeed pardon them if you not only grant them their lives but ensure that they shall not lose them.

11. Such was Augustus when an old man, or when growing old: in his youth he was hasty and passionate, and did many things upon which he looked back with regret. No one will venture to compare the rule of the blessed Augustus to the mildness of your own, even if your youth be compared with his more than ripe old age: he was gentle and placable, but it was after he had dyed the sea at Actium with Roman blood; after he had wrecked both the enemy's fleet and his own at Sicily; after the holocaust of Perusia and the proscriptions. But I do not call it clemency to be wearied of cruelty; true clemency, Caesar, is that which you display, which has not begun from remorse at its past ferocity, on which there is no stain, which has never shed the blood of your countrymen: this, when combined with unlimited power, shows the truest self-control and all-embracing love of the human race as of one's self, not corrupted by any low desires, any extravagant ideas, or any of the bad examples of former emperors into trying, by actual experiment, how great a tyranny you would be allowed to exercise over his countrymen, but inclining rather to blunting your sword of empire. You, Caesar, have granted us the boon of keeping our state free from bloodshed, and that of which you boast, that you have not caused one single drop of blood to flow in any part of the world, is all the more magnanimous and marvellous because no one ever had the power of the sword placed in his hands at an earlier age. Clemency, then, makes princes safer as well as

more respected, and is a glory to empires besides being their most trustworthy means of preservation. Why have legitimate sovereigns grown old on the throne, and bequeathed their power to their children and grandchildren, while the sway of despotic usurpers is both hateful and short-lived? What is the difference between the tyrant and the king— for their outward symbols of authority and their powers are the same—except it be that tyrants take delight in cruelty, whereas kings are only cruel for good reasons and because they cannot help it.

12. "What, then," say you, "do not kings also put men to death?" They do, but only when that measure is recommended by the public advantage: tyrants enjoy cruelty. A tyrant differs from a king in deeds, not in title: for the elder Dionysius deserves to be preferred before many kings, and what can prevent our styling Lucius Sulla a tyrant, since he only left off slaying because he had no more enemies to slay? Although he laid down his dictatorship and resumed the garb of a private citizen, yet what tyrant ever drank human blood as greedily as he, who ordered seven thousand Roman citizens to be butchered, and who, on hearing the shrieks of so many thousands being put to the sword as he sat in the temple of Bellona, said to the terror-stricken Senate, "Let us attend to our business, Conscript Fathers; it is only a few disturbers of the public peace who are being put to death by my orders." In saying this he did not lie: they really seemed few to Sulla. But we shall speak of Sulla presently, when we consider how we ought to feel anger against our enemies, at any rate when our own countrymen, members of the same community as ourselves, have been torn away from it and assumed the name of enemies: in the meanwhile, as I was saying, clemency is what makes the great distinction between kings and tyrants. Though each of them may be equally fenced around by armed soldiers, nevertheless the one uses his troops to safeguard the peace of his kingdom, the other uses them to

quell great hatred by great terror: and yet he does not look with any confidence upon those to whose hands he entrusts himself. He is driven in opposite directions by conflicting passions: for since he is hated because he is feared, he wishes to be feared because he is hated: and he acts up to the spirit of that odious verse, which has cast so many headlong from their thrones—

"Why, let them hate me, if they fear me too!"—

not knowing how frantic men become when their hatred becomes excessive: for a moderate amount of fear restrains men, but a constant and keen apprehension of the worst tortures rouses up even the most grovelling spirits to deeds of reckless courage, and causes them to hesitate at nothing. Just so a string stuck full of feathers will prevent wild beasts escaping: but should a horseman begin to shoot at them from another quarter, they will attempt to escape over the very thing that scared them, and will trample the cause of their alarm underfoot. No courage is so great as that which is born of utter desperation. In order to keep people down by terror, you must grant them a certain amount of security, and let them see that they have far more to hope for than to fear: for otherwise, if a man is in equal peril whether he sits still or takes action, he will feel actual pleasure in risking his life, and will fling it away as lightly as though it were not his own.

13. A calm and peaceful king trusts his guards, because he makes use of them to ensure the common safety of all his subjects, and his soldiers, who see that the security of the state depends upon their labours, cheerfully undergo the severest toil and glory in being the protectors of the father of their country: whereas your harsh and murderous tyrant must needs be disliked even by his own janissaries. No man can expect willing and loyal service from those whom he uses like the rack and the axe, as instruments of torture and death, to whom

he casts men as he would cast them to wild beasts. No prisoner at the bar is so full of agony and anxiety as a tyrant; for while he dreads both gods and men because they have witnessed, and will avenge his crimes, he has at the same time so far committed himself to this course of action that he is not able to alter it. This is perhaps the very worst quality of cruelty: a man must go on exercising it, and it is impossible for him to retrace his steps and start in a better path; for crimes must be safeguarded by fresh crimes. Yet who can be more unhappy than he who is actually compelled to be a villain? How greatly he ought to be pitied: I mean, by himself, for it would be impious for others to pity a man who has made use of his power to murder and ravage, who has rendered himself mistrusted by everyone at home and abroad, who fears the very soldiers to whom he flees for safety, who dares not rely upon the loyalty of his friends or the affection of his children: who, whenever he considers what he has done, and what he is about to do, and calls to mind all the crimes and torturings with which his conscience is burdened, must often fear death, and yet must often wish for it, for he must be even more hateful to himself than he is to his subjects. On the other hand, he who takes an interest in the entire state, who watches over every department of it with more or less care, who attends to all the business of the state as well as if it were his own, who is naturally inclined to mild measures, and shows, even when it is to his advantage to punish, how unwilling he is to make use of harsh remedies; who has no angry or savage feelings, but wields his authority calmly and beneficially, being anxious that even his subordinate officers shall be popular with his countrymen, who thinks his happiness complete if he can make the nation share his prosperity, who is courteous in language, whose presence is easy of access, who looks obligingly upon his subjects, who is disposed to grant all their reasonable wishes, and does not treat their unreasonable wishes with harshness—such a prince is loved, protected, and worshipped by his whole empire. Men talk of such a one in private in the same words which they use in public: they are eager to bring up families under his reign, and they put an end to the childlessness which public misery had previously rendered general: everyone feels that he will indeed deserve that his children should be grateful to him for having brought them into so happy an age. Such a prince is rendered safe by his own beneficence; he has no need of guards, their arms serve him merely as decorations.

14. What, then, is his duty? It is that of good parents, who sometimes scold their children good-naturedly, sometimes threaten them, and sometimes even flog them. No man in his senses disinherits his son for his first offence: he does not pass this extreme sentence upon him unless his patience has been worn out by many grievous wrongs, unless he fears that his son will do something worse than that which he punishes him for having done; before doing this he makes many attempts to lead his son's mind into the right way while it is still hesitating between good and evil and has only taken its first steps in depravity; it is only when its case is hopeless that he adopts this extreme measure. No one demands that people should be executed until after he has failed to reform them. This which is the duty of a parent, is also that of the prince whom with no unmeaning flattery we call "The Father of our Country." Other names are given as titles of honour: we have styled some men "The Great," "The Fortunate," or "The August," and have thus satisfied their passion for grandeur by bestowing upon them all the dignity that we could: but when we style a man "The Father of his Country" we give him to understand that we have entrusted him with a father's power over us, which is of the mildest character, for a father takes thought for his children and subordinates his own interests to theirs. It is long before a father will cut off a member of his own body: even after he has cut it off he longs to replace it, and in cutting it off he laments and hesitates much and long: for he who condemns quickly is not far from

being willing to condemn; and he who inflicts too great punishment comes very near to punishing unjustly.

15. Within my own recollection the people stabbed in the Forum with their writing-styles a Roman knight named Tricho, because he had flogged his son to death: even the authority of Augustus Caesar could hardly save him from the angry clutches of both fathers and sons: but everyone admired Tarius, who, on discovering that his son meditated parricide, tried him, convicted him, and was then satisfied with punishing him by exile, and that, too, to that pleasant place of exile, Marseilles, where he made him the same yearly allowance which he had done while he was innocent: the result of this generosity was that even in a city where every villain finds someone to defend him, no one doubted that he was justly condemned, since even the father who was unable to hate him, nevertheless had condemned him. In this very same instance I will give you an example of a good prince, which you may compare with a good father. Tarius, when about to sit in judgement on his son, invited Augustus Caesar to assist in trying him: Augustus came into his private house, sat beside the father, took part in another man's family council, and did not say, "Nay, let him rather come to my house," because if he had done so, the trial would have been conducted by Caesar and not by the father. When the cause had been heard, after all that the young man pleaded in his own defence and all that was alleged against him had been thoroughly discussed, the emperor begged that each man would write his sentence (instead of pronouncing it aloud), in order that they might not all follow Caesar in giving sentence: then, before the tablets were opened, he declared that if Tarius, who was a rich man, made him his heir, he would not accept the bequest. One might say "It showed a paltry mind in him to fear that people would think that he condemned the son in order to enable himself to inherit the estate." I am of a contrary opinion—any one of us ought to have sufficient

trust in the consciousness of his own integrity to defend him against calumny, but princes must take great pains to avoid even the appearance of evil. He swore that he would not accept the property. On that day Tarius lost two heirs to his estate, but Caesar gained the liberty of forming an unbiased judgement: and when he had proved that his severity was disinterested, a point of which a prince should never lose sight, he gave sentence that the son should be banished to whatever place the father might choose. He did not sentence him to the sack and the snakes, or to prison, because he thought, not of who it was upon whom he was passing sentence, but of who it was with whom he was sitting in judgement: he said that a father ought to be satisfied with the mildest form of punishment for his stripling son, who had been seduced into a crime which he had attempted so faintheartedly as to be almost innocent of it, and that he ought to be removed from Rome and out of his father's sight.

16. How worthy was he to be invited by fathers to join their family councils: how worthy to be made co-heir with innocent children! This is the sort of clemency which befits a prince; wherever he goes, let him make everyone more charitable. In the king's sight, no one ought to be so despicable that he should not notice whether he lives or dies: be his character what it may, he is a part of the empire. Let us take examples for great kingdoms from smaller ones. There are many forms of royalty: a prince reigns over his subjects, a father over his children, a teacher over his scholars, a tribune or centurion over his soldiers. Would not he, who constantly punished his children by beating them for the most trifling faults, be thought the worst of fathers? Which is worthier to impart a liberal education: he who flays his scholars alive if their memory be weak, or if their eyes do not run quickly along the lines as they read, or he who prefers to improve and instruct them by kindly warnings and moral influence? If a tribune or a centurion is harsh, he will make men deserters, and one

cannot blame them for desertion. It is never right to rule a human being more harshly and cruelly than we rule dumb animals; yet a skilled horse-breaker will not scare a horse by frequent blows, because he will become timid and vicious if you do not soothe him with pats and caresses. So also a huntsman, both when he is teaching puppies to follow the tracks of wild animals, and when he uses dogs already trained to drive them from their lairs and hunt them, does not often threaten to beat them, for, if he does, he will break their spirit, and make them stupid and currish with fear; though, on the other hand, he will not allow them to roam and range about unrestrained. The same is the case with those who drive the slower draught cattle, which, though brutal treatment and wretchedness is their lot from their birth, still, by excessive cruelty may be made to refuse to draw.

17. No creature is more self-willed, requires more careful management, or ought to be treated with greater indulgence than man. What, indeed, can be more foolish than that we should blush to show anger against dogs or beasts of burden, and yet wish one man to be most abominably ill-treated by another? We are not angry with diseases, but apply remedies to them: but this also is a disease of the mind, and requires soothing medicine and a physician who is anything but angry with his patient. It is the part of a bad physician to despair of effecting a cure: he, to whom the care of all men's well-being is entrusted, ought to act like a good physician, and not be in a hurry to give up hope or to declare that the symptoms are mortal: he should wrestle with vices, withstand them, reproach some with their distemper, and deceive others by a soothing mode of treatment, because he will cure his patient more quickly and more thoroughly if the medicines which he administers escape his notice: a prince should take care not only of the recovery of his people, but also that their scars should be honourable. Cruel punishments do a king no honour: for who doubts that he is able to inflict them? but, on

the other hand, it does him great honour to restrain his powers, to save many from the wrath of others, and sacrifice no one to his own.

18. It is creditable to a man to keep within reasonable bounds in his treatment of his slaves. Even in the case of a human chattel one ought to consider, not how much one can torture him with impunity, but how far such treatment is permitted by natural goodness and justice, which prompts us to act kindly towards even prisoners of war and slaves bought for a price (how much more towards free-born, respectable gentlemen?), and not to treat them with scornful brutality as human chattels, but as persons somewhat below ourselves in station, who have been placed under our protection rather than assigned to us as servants. Slaves are allowed to run and take sanctuary at the statue of a god, though the laws allow a slave to be ill-treated to any extent, there are nevertheless some things which the common laws of life forbid us to do to a human being. Who does not hate Vedius Pollio more even than his own slaves did, because he used to fatten his lampreys with human blood, and ordered those who had offended him in any way to be cast into his fish-pond, or rather snake-pond? That man deserved to die a thousand deaths, both for throwing his slaves to be devoured by the lampreys which he himself meant to eat, and for keeping lampreys that he might feed them in such a fashion. Cruel masters are pointed at with disgust in all parts of the city, and are hated and loathed; the wrong-doings of kings are enacted on a wider theatre: their shame and unpopularity endures for ages: yet how far better it would have been never to have been born than to be numbered among those who have been born to do their country harm!

19. Nothing can be imagined which is more becoming to a sovereign than clemency, by whatever title and right he may be set over his fellow citizens. The greater his power, the more

beautiful and admirable he will confess his clemency to be: for there is no reason why power should do any harm, if only it be wielded in accordance with the laws of nature. Nature herself has conceived the idea of a king, as you may learn from various animals, and especially from bees, among whom the king's cell is the roomiest, and is placed in the most central and safest part of the hive; moreover, he does no work, but employs himself in keeping the others up to their work. If the king be lost, the entire swarm disperses: they never endure to have more than one king at a time, and find out which is the better by making them fight with one another: moreover the king is distinguished by his statelier appearance, being both larger and more brilliantly coloured than the other bees. The most remarkable distinction, however, is the following: bees are very fierce, and for their size are the most pugnacious of creatures, and leave their stings in the wounds which they make, but the king himself has no sting: nature does not wish him to be savage or to seek revenge at so dear a rate, and so has deprived him of his weapon and disarmed his rage. She has offered him as a pattern to great sovereigns: for she is wont to practise herself in small matters, and to scatter abroad tiny models of the hugest structures. We ought to be ashamed of not learning a lesson in behaviour from these small creatures, for a man, who has so much more power of doing harm than they, ought to show a correspondingly greater amount of self-control. Would that human beings were subject to the same law, and that their anger destroyed itself together with its instrument, so that they could only inflict a wound once, and would not make use of the strength of others to carry out their hatreds: for their fury would soon grow faint if it carried its own punishment with it, and could only give rein to its violence at the risk of death. Even as it is, however, no one can exercise it with safety, for he must needs feel as much fear as he hopes to cause, he must watch everyone's movements, and even when his enemies are not laying violent hands upon him he must bear in mind that they are plotting to do so, and he cannot have a single moment free from alarm. Would anyone endure to live such a life as this, when he might enjoy the privileges of his high station to the general joy of all men, without injuring anyone, and for that very reason have no one to fear? for it is a mistake to suppose that the king can be safe in a state where nothing is safe from the king: he can only purchase a life without anxiety for himself by guaranteeing the same for his subjects. He need not pile up lofty citadels, escarp steep hills, cut away the sides of mountains, and fence himself about with many lines of walls and towers: clemency will render a king safe even upon an open plain. The one fortification which cannot be stormed is the love of his countrymen. What can be more glorious than a life which everyone spontaneously and without official pressure hopes may last long? to excite men's fears, not their hopes, if one's health gives way a little? to know that no one holds anything so dear that he would not be glad to give it in exchange for the health of his sovereign? "O, may no evil befall him!" they would cry: "he must live for his own sake, not only for ours: his constant proofs of goodness have made him belong to the state instead of the state belonging to him." Who would dare to plot any danger to such a king? Who would not rather, if he could, keep misfortune far from one under whom justice, peace, decency, security, and merit flourish, under whom the state grows rich with an abundance of all good things, and looks upon its ruler in the same spirit of adoration and respect with which we should look upon the immortal gods, if they allowed us to behold them as we behold him? Why! does not that man come very close to the gods who acts in a god-like manner, and who is beneficent, open-handed, and powerful for good? Your aim and your pride ought to lie in being thought the best, as well as the greatest of mankind.

20. A prince generally inflicts punishment for one of two reasons: he wishes either to assert his own rights or those of

another. I will first discuss the case in which he is personally concerned, for it is more difficult for him to act with
moderation when he acts under the impulse of actual pain
than when he merely does so for the sake of the example.
It is unnecessary in this place to remind him to be slow to
believe what he hears, to ferret out the truth, to show favour
to innocence, and to bear in mind that to prove it is as much
the business of the judge as that of the prisoner; for these
considerations are connected with justice, not with clemency:
what we are now encouraging him to do is not to lose control
over his feelings when he receives an unmistakeable injury,
and to forego punishing it if he possibly can do so with safety,
if not, to moderate the severity of the punishment, and to
show himself far more unwilling to forgive wrongs done to
others than those done to himself: for, just as the truly generous man is not he who gives away what belongs to others, but
he who deprives himself of what he gives to another, so also I
should not call a prince clement who looked good-naturedly
upon a wrong done to someone else, but one who is unmoved
even by the sting of a personal injury, who understands how
magnanimous it is for one whose power is unlimited to allow
himself to be wronged, and that there is no more noble spectacle than that of a sovereign who has received an injury
without avenging it.

21. Vengeance effects two purposes: it either affords compensation to the person to whom the wrong was done, or it ensures
him against molestation for the future. A prince is too rich
to need compensation, and his power is too evident for him
to require to gain a reputation for power by causing anyone to suffer. I mean, when he is attacked and injured by his
inferiors, for if he sees those who once were his equals in a
position of inferiority to himself he is sufficiently avenged.
A king may be killed by a slave, or a serpent, or an arrow:
but no one can be saved except by someone who is greater
than him whom he saves. He, therefore, who has the power

of giving and of taking away life ought to use such a great gift of heaven in a spirited manner. Above all, if he once obtains this power over those who he knows were once on a level with himself, he has completed his revenge, and done all that he need to towards the punishment of his adversary: for he who owes his life to another must have lost it, and he who has been cast down from on high and lies at his enemy's feet with his kingdom and his life depending upon the pleasure of another, adds to the glory of his preserver if he be allowed to live, and increases his reputation much more by remaining unhurt than if he were put out of the way. In the former case he remains as an everlasting testimony to the valour of his conqueror; whereas if led in the procession of a triumph he would have soon passed out of sight. If, however, his kingdom also may be safely left in his hands and he himself replaced upon the throne from which he has fallen, such a measure confers an immense increase of lustre on him who scorned to take anything from a conquered king beyond the glory of having conquered him. To do this is to triumph even over one's own victory, and to declare that one has found nothing among the vanquished which it was worth the victor's while to take. As for his countrymen, strangers, and persons of mean condition, he ought to treat them with all the less severity because it costs so much less to overcome them. Some you would be glad to spare, against some you would disdain to assert your rights, and would forbear to touch them as you would to touch little insects which defile your hands when you crush them: but in the case of men upon whom all eyes are fixed, whether they be spared or condemned, you should seize the opportunity of making your clemency widely known.

22. Let us now pass on to the consideration of wrongs done to others, in avenging which the law has aimed at three ends, which the prince will do well to aim at also: they are, either that it may correct him whom it punishes, or that his

punishment may render other men better, or that, by bad
men being put out of the way, the rest may live without fear.
You will more easily correct the men themselves by a slight
punishment, for he who has some part of his fortune remaining untouched will behave less recklessly; on the other hand,
no one cares about respectability after he has lost it: it is a
species of impunity to have nothing left for punishment
to take away. It is conducive, however, to good morals in a
state, that punishment should seldom be inflicted: for where
there is a multitude of sinners men become familiar with sin,
shame is less felt when shared with a number of fellow criminals, and severe sentences, if frequently pronounced, lose
the influence which constitutes their chief power as remedial
measures. A good king establishes a good standard of morals
for his kingdom and drives away vices if he is long-suffering
with them, not that he should seem to encourage them, but
to be very unwilling and to suffer much when he is forced
to chastise them. Clemency in a sovereign even makes men
ashamed to do wrong: for punishment seems far more grievous when inflicted by a merciful man.

23. Besides this, you will find that sins which are frequently
punished are frequently committed. Your father sewed up
more parricides in sacks during five years, than we hear of
in all previous centuries. As long as the greatest of crimes
remained without any special law, children were much more
timid about committing it. Our wise ancestors, deeply skilled
in human nature, preferred to pass over this as being a
wickedness too great for belief, and beyond the audacity of
the worst criminal, rather than teach men that it might be
done by appointing a penalty for doing it: parricides, conse-
quently, were unknown until a law was made against them,
and the penalty showed them the way to the crime. Filial
affection soon perished, for since that time we have seen
more men punished by the sack than by the cross. Where
men are seldom punished innocence becomes the rule, and

is encouraged as a public benefit. If a state thinks itself innocent, it will be innocent: it will be all the more angry with
those who corrupt the general simplicity of manners if it
sees that they are few in number. Believe me, it is a dangerous thing to show a state how great a majority of bad men
it contains.

24. A proposal was once made in the Senate to distinguish slaves
from free men by their dress: it was then discovered how
dangerous it would be for our slaves to be able to count our
numbers. Be assured that the same thing would be the case
if no one's offence is pardoned: it will quickly be discovered
how far the number of bad men exceeds that of the good.
Many executions are as disgraceful to a sovereign as many
funerals are to a physician: one who governs less strictly is
better obeyed. The human mind is naturally self-willed, kicks
against the goad, and sets its face against authority; it will
follow more readily than it can be led. As well-bred and high-
spirited horses are best managed with a loose rein, so mercy
gives men's minds a spontaneous bias towards innocence,
and the public thinks that it is worth observing. Mercy, therefore, does more good than severity.

25. Cruelty is far from being a human vice, and is unworthy of
man's gentle mind: it is mere bestial madness to take pleasure
in blood and wounds, to cast off humanity and transform
oneself into a wild beast of the forest. Pray, Alexander, what
is the difference between your throwing Lysimachus into
a lion's den and tearing his flesh with your own teeth? it is
you that have the lion's maw, and the lion's fierceness. How
pleased you would be if you had claws instead of nails, and
jaws that were capable of devouring men! We do not expect
of you that your hand, the sure murderer of your best friends,
should restore health to anyone; or that your proud spirit,
that inexhaustible source of evil to all nations, should be satisfied with anything short of blood and slaughter: we rather

call it mercy that your friend should have a human being chosen to be his butcher. The reason why cruelty is the most hateful of all vices is that it goes first beyond the ordinary limits, and then beyond those of humanity; that it devises new kinds of punishments, calls ingenuity to aid it in inventing devices for varying and lengthening men's torture, and takes delight in their sufferings: this accursed disease of the mind reaches its highest pitch of madness when cruelty itself turns into pleasure, and the act of killing a man becomes enjoyment. Such a ruler is soon cast down from his throne; his life is attempted by poison one day and by the sword the next; he is exposed to as many dangers as there are men to whom he is dangerous, and he is sometimes destroyed by the plots of individuals, and at others by a general insurrection. Whole communities are not roused to action by unimportant outrages on private persons; but cruelty which takes a wider range, and from which no one is safe, becomes a mark for all men's weapons. Very small snakes escape our notice, and the whole country does not combine to destroy them; but when one of them exceeds the usual size and grows into a monster, when it poisons fountains with its spittle, scorches herbage with its breath, and spreads ruin wherever it crawls, we shoot at it with military engines. Trifling evils may cheat us and elude our observation, but we gird up our loins to attack great ones. One sick person does not so much as disquiet the house in which he lies; but when frequent deaths show that a plague is raging, there is a general outcry, men take to flight and shake their fists angrily at the very gods themselves. If a fire breaks out under one single roof, the family and the neighbours pour water upon it; but a wide conflagration which has consumed many houses must be smothered under the ruins of a whole quarter of a city.

26. The cruelty even of private men has sometimes been revenged by their slaves in spite of the certainty that they will be crucified: whole kingdoms and nations when oppressed

by tyrants or threatened by them, have attempted their destruction. Sometimes their own guards have risen in revolt, and have used against their master all the deceit, disloyalty, and ferocity which they have learned from him. What, indeed, can he expect from those whom he has taught to be wicked? A bad man will not long be obedient, and will not do only as much evil as he is ordered. But even if the tyrant may be cruel with safety, how miserable his kingdom must be: it must look like a city taken by storm, like some frightful scene of general panic. Everywhere sorrow, anxiety, disorder; men dread even their own pleasures; they cannot even dine with one another in safety when they have to keep watch over their tongues even when in their cups, nor can they safely attend the public shows when informers are ready to find grounds for their impeachment in their behaviour there. Although the spectacles be provided at an enormous expense, with royal magnificence and with world-famous artists, yet who cares for amusement when he is in prison? Ye gods! what a miserable life it is to slaughter and to rage, to delight in the clanking of chains, and to cut off one's countrymen's heads, to cause blood to flow freely wherever one goes, to terrify people, and make them flee away out of one's sight! It is what would happen if bears or lions were our masters, if serpents and all the most venomous creatures were given power over us. Even these animals, devoid of reason as they are, and accused by us of cruel ferocity, spare their own kind, and wild beasts themselves respect their own likeness: but the fury of tyrants does not even stop short at their own relations, and they treat friends and strangers alike, only becoming more violent the more they indulge their passions. By insensible degrees he proceeds from the slaughter of individuals to the ruin of nations, and thinks it a sign of power to set roofs on fire and to plough up the sites of ancient cities: he considers it unworthy of an emperor to order only one or two people to be put to death, and thinks that his cruelty is unduly restrained if whole troops of wretches are not sent to execution together.

True happiness, on the other hand, consists in saving many men's lives, in calling them back from the very gates of death, and in being so merciful as to deserve a civic crown. No decoration is more worthy or more becoming to a prince's rank than that crown "for saving the lives of fellow-citizens": not trophies torn from a vanquished enemy, not chariots wet with their savage owner's blood, not spoils captured in war. This power which saves men's lives by crowds and by nations, is godlike: the power of extensive and indiscriminate massacre is the power of downfall and conflagration.

Part II

1. I have been especially led to write about clemency, Nero Caesar, by a saying of yours, which I remember having heard with admiration and which I afterwards told to others: a noble saying, showing a great mind and great gentleness, which suddenly burst from you without premeditation, and was not meant to reach any ears but your own, and which displayed the conflict which was raging between your natural goodness and your imperial duties. Your prefect Burrus, an excellent man who was born to be the servant of such an emperor as you are, was about to order two brigands to be executed, and was pressing you to write their names and the grounds on which they were to be put to death: this had often been put off, and he was insisting that it should then be done. When he reluctantly produced the document and put it into your equally reluctant hands, you exclaimed: "Would that I had never learned my letters!" O what a speech, how worthy to be heard by all nations, both those who dwell within the Roman Empire, those who enjoy a debatable independence upon its borders, and those who either in will or in deed fight against it! It is a speech which ought to be spoken before a meeting of all mankind, whose words all kings and princes ought to swear to obey: a speech worthy of the days of human

innocence, and worthy to bring back that golden age. Now in truth we ought all to agree to love righteousness and goodness; covetousness, which is the root of all evil, ought to be driven away, piety and virtue, good faith and modesty ought to resume their interrupted reign, and the vices which have so long and so shamefully ruled us ought at last to give way to an age of happiness and purity.

2. To a great extent, Caesar, we may hope and expect that this will come to pass. Let your own goodness of heart be gradually spread and diffused throughout the whole body of the empire, and all parts of it will mould themselves into your likeness. Good health proceeds from the head into all the members of the body: they are all either brisk and erect, or languid and drooping, according as their guiding spirit blooms or withers. Both Romans and allies will prove worthy of this goodness of yours, and good morals will return to all the world: your hands will everywhere find less to do. Allow me to dwell somewhat upon this saying of yours, not because it is a pleasant subject for your ears (indeed, this is not my way; I would rather offend by telling the truth than curry favour by flattery). What, then, is my reason? Besides wishing that you should be as familiar as possible with your own good deeds and good words, in order that what is now untutored impulse may grow into matured decision, I remember that many great but odious sayings have become part of human life and are familiar in men's mouths, such as that celebrated "Let them hate me, provided that they fear me," which is like that Greek verse in which a man bids the earth perish in flame after he is dead, and others of the like sort. I know not how it is, but certainly human ingenuity seems to have found it easier to find emphatic and ardent expression for monstrous and cynical sentiments: I have never hitherto heard any spirited saying from a good and gentle person. What, then, is the upshot of all this? It is that, albeit seldom and against your will, and after much hesitation, you sometimes

nevertheless must write that which made you hate your letters, but that you ought to do so with great hesitation and after many postponements, even as you now do.

3. But lest the plausible word "mercy" should sometimes deceive us and lead us into the opposite extreme, let us consider what mercy is, what its qualities are, and within what limits it is confined.

Mercy is "a restraining of the mind from vengeance when it is in its power to avenge itself," or it is "gentleness shown by a powerful man in fixing the punishment of a weaker one." It is safer to have more than one definition, since one may not include the whole subject, and may, so to speak, lose its cause: mercy, therefore, may likewise be termed a tendency towards mildness in inflicting punishment. It is possible to discover certain inconsistencies in the definition which comes nearer the truth than all the rest, which is to call mercy "self-restraint, which remits some part of a fine which it deserves to receive and which is due to it." To this it will be objected that no virtue ever gives any man less than his due. However, all men understand mercy to consist in coming short of the penalty which might with justice be inflicted.

4. The unlearned think that its opposite is strictness: but no virtue is the opposite of another virtue. What, then, is the opposite of mercy? Cruelty: which is nothing more than obstinacy in exacting punishments. "But," say you, "some men do not exact punishments, and nevertheless are cruel, such as those who kill the strangers whom they meet, not in order to rob them, but for killing's sake, and men who are not satisfied with killing, but kill with savage tortures, like the famous Busiris, and Procrustes, and pirates who flog their captives and burn them alive." This appears to be cruelty: but as it is not the result of vengeance (for it has received no wrong), and is not excited by any offence (for no crime has preceded it), it does not come within our definition, which was limited

to "extravagance in exacting the penalties of wrongdoing." We may say that this is not cruelty, but ferocity, which finds pleasure in savagery: or we may call it madness; for madness is of various kinds, and there is no truer madness than that which takes to slaughtering and mutilating human beings. I shall, therefore, call those persons cruel who have a reason for punishing but who punish without moderation, like Phalaris, who is not said to have tortured innocent men, but to have tortured criminals with inhuman and incredible barbarity. We may avoid hairsplitting by defining cruelty to be "a tendency of the mind towards harsh measures." Mercy repels cruelty and bids it be far from her: with strictness she is on terms of amity.

At this point it is useful to inquire into what pity is; for many praise it as a virtue, and say that a good man is full of pity. This also is a disease of the mind. Both of these stand close to mercy and to strictness, and both ought to be avoided, lest under the name of strictness we be led into cruelty, and under the name of mercy into pity. It is less dangerous to make the latter mistake, but both lead us equally far away from the truth.

5. Just as the gods are worshipped by religion, but are dishonoured by superstition, so all good men will show mercy and mildness, but will avoid pity, which is a vice incident to weak minds which cannot endure the sight of another's sufferings. It is, therefore, most commonly found in the worst people; there are old women and girls who are affected by the tears of the greatest criminals, and who, if they could, would let them out of prison. Pity considers a man's misfortunes and does not consider to what they are due: mercy is combined with reason. I know that the doctrine of the Stoics is unpopular among the ignorant as being excessively severe and not at all likely to give kings and princes good advice; it is blamed because it declares that the wise man knows not how to feel pity or to grant pardon. These doctrines, if taken

separately, are indeed odious, for they appear to give men no hope of repairing their mistakes but exact a penalty for every slip. If this were true, how can it be true wisdom to bid us put off human feeling, and to exclude us from mutual help, that surest haven of refuge against the attacks of Fortune? But no school of philosophy is more gentle and benignant, none is more full of love towards man or more anxious to promote the happiness of all, seeing that its maxims are, to be of service and assistance to others, and to consult the interests of each and all, not of itself alone. Pity is a disorder of the mind caused by the sight of other men's miseries, or it is a sadness caused by the evils with which it believes others to be undeservedly afflicted: but the wise man cannot be affected by any disorder: his mind is calm, and nothing can possibly happen to ruffle it. Moreover, nothing becomes a man more than magnanimity: but magnanimity cannot coexist with sorrow. Sorrow overwhelms men's minds, casts them down, contracts them: now this cannot happen to the wise man even in his greatest misfortunes, but he will beat back the rage of Fortune and triumph over it: he will always retain the same calm, undisturbed expression of countenance, which he never could do were he accessible to sorrow.

6. Add to this, that the wise man provides for the future and always has a distinct plan of action ready: yet nothing clear and true can flow from a disturbed source. Sorrow is awkward at reviewing the position of affairs, at devising useful expedients, avoiding dangerous courses, and weighing the merits of fair and just ones: therefore the wise man will not feel pity, because this cannot happen to a man unless his mind is disturbed. He will do willingly and highmindedly all that those who feel pity are wont to do; he will dry the tears of others, but will not mingle his own with them; he will stretch out his hand to the shipwrecked mariner, will offer hospitality to the exile, and alms to the needy—not in the offensive way in which most of those who wish to be thought tenderhearted

fling their bounty to those whom they assist and shrink from their touch, but as one man would give another something out of the common stock—he will restore children to their weeping mothers, will loose the chains of the captive, release the gladiator from his bondage, and even bury the carcase of the criminal, but he will perform all this with a calm mind and unaltered expression of countenance. Thus the wise man will not pity men, but will help them and be of service to them, seeing that he is born to be a help to all men and a public benefit, of which he will bestow a share upon every one. He will even grant a proportional part of his bounty to those sufferers who deserve blame and correction; but he will much more willingly help those whose troubles and adversities are caused by misfortune. Whenever he is able he will interpose between Fortune and her victims: for what better employment can he find for his wealth or his strength than in setting up again what chance has overthrown? He will not show or feel any disgust at a man's having withered legs, or a flabby wrinkled skin, or supporting his aged body upon a staff; but he will do good to those who deserve it, and will, like a god, look benignantly upon all who are in trouble. Pity borders upon misery: it is partly composed of it and partly derived from it. You know that eyes must be weak, if they fill with rheum at the sight of another's blearedness, just as it is not real merriment but hysteria which makes people laugh because others laugh, and yawn whenever others open their jaws: pity is a defect in the mind of people who are extraordinarily affected by suffering, and he who requires a wise man to exhibit it is not far from requiring him to lament and groan when strangers are buried.

7. But why should he not pardon? Let us decide by exact definition this other slippery matter, the true nature of pardon, and we shall then perceive that the wise man ought not to grant it. Pardon is the remitting of a deserved punishment. The reasons why the wise man ought not to grant this remission

are given at length by those of whom this question is specially asked: I will briefly say, as though it were no concern of mine to decide this point, "A man grants pardon to one whom he ought to punish: now the wise man does nothing which he ought not to do, and omits to do nothing which he ought to do: he does not, therefore, remit any punishment which he ought to exact. But the wise man will bestow upon you in a more honourable way that which you wish to obtain by pardon, for he will make allowances for you, will consult your interests, and will correct your bad habits: he will act just as though he were pardoning you, but nevertheless he will not pardon you, because he who pardons admits that in so doing he has neglected a part of his duty. He will only punish some people by reprimanding them, and will inflict no further penalty if he considers that they are of an age which admits of reformation: some people who are undeniably implicated in an odious charge he will acquit, because they were deceived into committing, or were not sober when they committed the offence with which they are charged: he will let his enemies depart unharmed, sometimes even with words of commendation, if they have taken up arms to defend their honour, their covenants with others, their freedom, or on any other honourable ground. All these doings come under the head of mercy, not of pardon. Mercy is free to come to what decision it pleases: she gives her decision, not under any statute, but according to equity and goodness: she may acquit the defendant, or impose what damages she pleases. She does not do any of these things as though she were doing less than justice requires, but as though the justest possible course were that which she adopts. On the other hand, to pardon is not to punish a man whom you have decided ought to be punished; pardon is the remission of a punishment which ought to be inflicted. The first advantage which mercy has over it is that she does not tell those whom she lets off that they ought to have suffered: she is more complete, more honourable than pardon."

In my opinion, this is a mere dispute about words, and we are agreed about the thing itself. The wise man will remit many penalties, and will save many who are wicked, but whose wickedness is not incurable. He will act like good husbandmen, who do not cultivate only straight and tall trees, but also apply props to straighten those which have been rendered crooked by various causes; they trim some, lest the luxuriance of their boughs should hinder their upward growth, they nurse those which have been weakened by being planted in an unsuitable position, and they give air to those which are overshadowed by the foliage of others. The wise man will see the several treatments suitable to several dispositions, and how what is crooked may be straightened. . . .

SELECTED LETTERS
FROM A STOIC

Translated by Richard M. Gummere, Ph.D.

ON SAVING TIME

Greetings from Seneca to his friend Lucilius.

1. Continue to act thus, my dear Lucilius—set yourself free for
   your own sake; gather and save your time, which till lately
   has been forced from you, or filched away, or has merely
   slipped from your hands. Make yourself believe the truth
   of my words,—that certain moments are torn from us, that
   some are gently removed, and that others glide beyond our
   reach. The most disgraceful kind of loss, however, is that
   due to carelessness. Furthermore, if you will pay close heed
   to the problem, you will find that the largest portion of our
   life passes while we are doing ill, a goodly share while we are
   doing nothing, and the whole while we are doing that which
   is not to the purpose.

2. What man can you show me who places any value on his time,
   who reckons the worth of each day, who understands that he
   is dying daily? For we are mistaken when we look forward
   to death; the major portion of death has already passed.
   Whatever years lie behind us are in death's hands.

   Therefore, Lucilius, do as you write me that you are doing:
   hold every hour in your grasp. Lay hold of to-day's task, and

you will not need to depend so much upon to-morrow's. While we are postponing, life speeds by.

3. Nothing, Lucilius, is ours, except time. We were entrusted by nature with the ownership of this single thing, so fleeting and slippery that anyone who will can oust us from possession. What fools these mortals be! They allow the cheapest and most useless things, which can easily be replaced, to be charged in the reckoning, after they have acquired them; but they never regard themselves as in debt when they have received some of that precious commodity,—time! And yet time is the one loan which even a grateful recipient cannot repay.

4. You may desire to know how I, who preach to you so freely, am practising. I confess frankly: my expense account balances, as you would expect from one who is free-handed but careful. I cannot boast that I waste nothing, but I can at least tell you what I am wasting, and the cause and manner of the loss; I can give you the reasons why I am a poor man. My situation, however, is the same as that of many who are reduced to slender means through no fault of their own: everyone forgives them, but no one comes to their rescue.

5. What is the state of things, then? It is this: I do not regard a man as poor, if the little which remains is enough for him. I advise you, however, to keep what is really yours; and you cannot begin too early. For, as our ancestors believed, it is too late to spare when you reach the dregs of the cask. Of that which remains at the bottom, the amount is slight, and the quality is vile. Farewell.

ON TRUE AND
FALSE FRIENDSHIP

1. You have sent a letter to me through the hand of a "friend" of yours, as you call him. And in your very next sentence you warn me not to discuss with him all the matters that concern you, saying that even you yourself are not accustomed to do this; in other words, you have in the same letter affirmed and denied that he is your friend.

2. Now if you used this word of ours in the popular sense, and called him "friend" in the same way in which we speak of all candidates for election as "honourable gentlemen," and as we greet all men whom we meet casually, if their names slip us for the moment, with the salutation "my dear sir,"—so be it. But if you consider any man a friend whom you do not trust as you trust yourself, you are mightily mistaken and you do not sufficiently understand what true friendship means. Indeed, I would have you discuss everything with a friend; but first of all discuss the man himself. When friendship is settled, you must trust; before friendship is formed, you must pass judgment. Those persons indeed put last first and confound their duties, who, violating the rules of Theophrastus, judge a man after they have made him their friend, instead of making him their friend after they have judged him. Ponder

for a long time whether you shall admit a given person to your friendship; but when you have decided to admit him, welcome him with all your heart and soul. Speak as boldly with him as with yourself.

3. As to yourself, although you should live in such a way that you trust your own self with nothing which you could not entrust even to your enemy, yet, since certain matters occur which convention keeps secret, you should share with a friend at least all your worries and reflections. Regard him as loyal, and you will make him loyal. Some, for example, fearing to be deceived, have taught men to deceive; by their suspicions they have given their friend the right to do wrong. Why need I keep back any words in the presence of my friend? Why should I not regard myself as alone when in his company?

4. There is a class of men who communicate, to anyone whom they meet, matters which should be revealed to friends alone, and unload upon the chance listener whatever irks them. Others, again, fear to confide in their closest intimates; and if it were possible, they would not trust even themselves, burying their secrets deep in their hearts. But we should do neither. It is equally faulty to trust everyone and to trust no one. Yet the former fault is, I should say, the more ingenuous, the latter the more safe.

5. In like manner you should rebuke these two kinds of men,—both those who always lack repose, and those who are always in repose. For love of bustle is not industry,—it is only the restlessness of a hunted mind. And true repose does not consist in condemning all motion as merely vexation; that kind of repose is slackness and inertia.

6. Therefore, you should note the following saying, taken from my reading in Pomponius: "Some men shrink into dark

corners, to such a degree that they see darkly by day." No, men should combine these tendencies, and he who reposes should act and he who acts should take repose. Discuss the problem with Nature; she will tell you that she has created both day and night. Farewell.

ON THE TERRORS OF DEATH

1. Keep on as you have begun, and make all possible haste, so that you may have longer enjoyment of an improved mind, one that is at peace with itself. Doubtless you will derive enjoyment during the time when you are improving your mind and setting it at peace with itself; but quite different is the pleasure which comes from contemplation when one's mind is so cleansed from every stain that it shines.

2. You remember, of course, what joy you felt when you laid aside the garments of boyhood and donned the man's toga, and were escorted to the Forum; nevertheless, you may look for a still greater joy when you have laid aside the mind of boyhood and when wisdom has enrolled you among men. For it is not boyhood that still stays with us, but something worse,—boyishness. And this condition is all the more serious because we possess the authority of old age, together with the follies of boyhood, yea, even the follies of infancy. Boys fear trifles, children fear shadows, we fear both.

3. All you need to do is to advance; you will thus understand that some things are less to be dreaded, precisely because they inspire us with great fear. No evil is great which is the last evil of all. Death arrives; it would be a thing to dread, if it

could remain with you. But death must either not come at all, or else must come and pass away.

4. "It is difficult, however," you say, "to bring the mind to a point where it can scorn life." But do you not see what trifling reasons impel men to scorn life? One hangs himself before the door of his mistress; another hurls himself from the housetop that he may no longer be compelled to bear the taunts of a bad-tempered master; a third, to be saved from arrest after running away, drives a sword into his vitals. Do you not suppose that virtue will be as efficacious as excessive fear? No man can have a peaceful life who thinks too much about lengthening it, or believes that living through many consulships is a great blessing.

5. Rehearse this thought every day, that you may be able to depart from life contentedly; for many men clutch and cling to life, even as those who are carried down a rushing stream clutch and cling to briars and sharp rocks.

Most men ebb and flow in wretchedness between the fear of death and the hardships of life; they are unwilling to live, and yet they do not know how to die.

6. For this reason, make life as a whole agreeable to yourself by banishing all worry about it. No good thing renders its possessor happy, unless his mind is reconciled to the possibility of loss; nothing, however, is lost with less discomfort than that which, when lost, cannot be missed. Therefore, encourage and toughen your spirit against the mishaps that afflict even the most powerful.

7. For example, the fate of Pompey was settled by a boy and a eunuch, that of Crassus by a cruel and insolent Parthian. Gaius Caesar ordered Lepidus to bare his neck for the axe of the tribune Dexter; and he himself offered his own throat to Chaerea. No man has ever been so far advanced by Fortune

that she did not threaten him as greatly as she had previously indulged him. Do not trust her seeming calm; in a moment the sea is moved to its depths. The very day the ships have made a brave show in the games, they are engulfed.

8. Reflect that a highwayman or an enemy may cut your throat; and, though he is not your master, every slave wields the power of life and death over you. Therefore I declare to you: he is lord of your life that scorns his own. Think of those who have perished through plots in their own homes, slain either openly or by guile; you will then understand that just as many have been killed by angry slaves as by angry kings. What matter, therefore, how powerful he be whom you fear, when every one possesses the power which inspires your fear?

9. "But," you will say, "if you should chance to fall into the hands of the enemy, the conqueror will command that you be led away,"—yes, whither you are already being led. Why do you voluntarily deceive yourself and require to be told now for the first time what fate it is that you have long been labouring under? Take my word for it: since the day you were born you are being led thither. We must ponder this thought, and thoughts of the like nature, if we desire to be calm as we await that last hour, the fear of which makes all previous hours uneasy.

10. But I must end my letter. Let me share with you the saying which pleased me to-day. It, too, is culled from another man's Garden: "Poverty brought into conformity with the law of nature, is great wealth." Do you know what limits that law of nature ordains for us? Merely to avert hunger, thirst, and cold. In order to banish hunger and thirst, it is not necessary for you to pay court at the doors of the purse-proud, or to submit to the stern frown, or to the kindness that humiliates; nor is it necessary for you to scour the seas, or go campaigning; nature's needs are easily provided and ready to hand.

11. It is the superfluous things for which men sweat,—the superfluous things that wear our togas threadbare, that force us
to grow old in camp, that dash us upon foreign shores. That
which is enough is ready to our hands. He who has made a
fair compact with poverty is rich. Farewell.

ON CROWDS

1. Do you ask me what you should regard as especially to be avoided? I say, crowds; for as yet you cannot trust yourself to them with safety. I shall admit my own weakness, at any rate; for I never bring back home the same character that I took abroad with me. Something of that which I have forced to be calm within me is disturbed; some of the foes that I have routed return again. Just as the sick man, who has been weak for a long time, is in such a condition that he cannot be taken out of the house without suffering a relapse, so we ourselves are affected when our souls are recovering from a lingering disease.

2. To consort with the crowd is harmful; there is no person who does not make some vice attractive to us, or stamp it upon us, or taint us unconsciously therewith. Certainly, the greater the mob with which we mingle, the greater the danger.

    But nothing is so damaging to good character as the habit of lounging at the games; for then it is that vice steals subtly upon one through the avenue of pleasure.

3. What do you think I mean? I mean that I come home more greedy, more ambitious, more voluptuous, and even more cruel and inhuman,—because I have been among human

beings. By chance I attended a mid-day exhibition, expecting some fun, wit, and relaxation,—an exhibition at which men's eyes have respite from the slaughter of their fellow-men. But it was quite the reverse. The previous combats were the essence of compassion; but now all the trifling is put aside and it is pure murder. The men have no defensive armour. They are exposed to blows at all points, and no one ever strikes in vain.

4. Many persons prefer this programme to the usual pairs and to the bouts "by request." Of course they do; there is no helmet or shield to deflect the weapon. What is the need of defensive armour, or of skill? All these mean delaying death. In the morning they throw men to the lions and the bears; at noon, they throw them to the spectators. The spectators demand that the slayer shall face the man who is to slay him in his turn; and they always reserve the latest conqueror for another butchering. The outcome of every fight is death, and the means are fire and sword. This sort of thing goes on while the arena is empty.

5. You may retort: "But he was a highway robber; he killed a man!" And what of it? Granted that, as a murderer, he deserved this punishment, what crime have you committed, poor fellow, that you should deserve to sit and see this show? In the morning they cried "Kill him! Lash him! Burn him! Why does he meet the sword in so cowardly a way? Why does he strike so feebly? Why doesn't he die game? Whip him to meet his wounds! Let them receive blow for blow, with chests bare and exposed to the stroke!" And when the games stop for the intermission, they announce: "A little throat-cutting in the meantime, so that there may still be something going on!"

Come, now; do you not understand even this truth, that a bad example reacts on the agent? Thank the immortal gods that you are teaching cruelty to a person who cannot learn to be cruel.

6.   The young character, which cannot hold fast to righteousness, must be rescued from the mob; it is too easy to side with the majority. Even Socrates, Cato, and Laelius might have been shaken in their moral strength by a crowd that was unlike them; so true it is that none of us, no matter how much he cultivates his abilities, can withstand the shock of faults that approach, as it were, with so great a retinue.

7.   Much harm is done by a single case of indulgence or greed; the familiar friend, if he be luxurious, weakens and softens us imperceptibly; the neighbour, if he be rich, rouses our covetousness; the companion, if he be slanderous, rubs off some of his rust upon us, even though we be spotless and sincere. What then do you think the effect will be on character, when the world at large assaults it! You must either imitate or loathe the world.

8.   But both courses are to be avoided; you should not copy the bad simply because they are many, nor should you hate the many because they are unlike you. Withdraw into yourself, as far as you can. Associate with those who will make a better man of you. Welcome those whom you yourself can improve. The process is mutual; for men learn while they teach.

9.   There is no reason why pride in advertising your abilities should lure you into publicity, so that you should desire to recite or harangue before the general public. Of course I should be willing for you to do so if you had a stock-in-trade that suited such a mob; as it is, there is not a man of them who can understand you. One or two individuals will perhaps come in your way, but even these will have to be moulded and trained by you so that they will understand you. You may say: "For what purpose did I learn all these things?" But you need not fear that you have wasted your efforts; it was for yourself that you learned them.

10. In order, however, that I may not to-day have learned exclusively for myself, I shall share with you three excellent sayings, of the same general purport, which have come to my attention. This letter will give you one of them as payment of my debt; the other two you may accept as a contribution in advance. Democritus says: "One man means as much to me as a multitude, and a multitude only as much as one man."

11. The following also was nobly spoken by someone or other, for it is doubtful who the author was; they asked him what was the object of all this study applied to an art that would reach but very few. He replied: "I am content with few, content with one, content with none at all." The third saying—and a noteworthy one, too—is by Epicurus, written to one of the partners of his studies: "I write this not for the many, but for you; each of us is enough of an audience for the other."

12. Lay these words to heart, Lucilius, that you may scorn the pleasure which comes from the applause of the majority. Many men praise you; but have you any reason for being pleased with yourself, if you are a person whom the many can understand? Your good qualities should face inwards. Farewell.

ON GROUNDLESS FEARS

1. I know that you have plenty of spirit; for even before you
   began to equip yourself with maxims which were wholesome
   and potent to overcome obstacles, you were taking pride in
   your contest with Fortune; and this is all the more true, now
   that you have grappled with Fortune and tested your powers. For our powers can never inspire in us implicit faith in
   ourselves except when many difficulties have confronted us
   on this side and on that, and have occasionally even come to
   close quarters with us. It is only in this way that the true spirit
   can be tested,—the spirit that will never consent to come
   under the jurisdiction of things external to ourselves.

2. This is the touchstone of such a spirit; no prizefighter can go
   with high spirits into the strife if he has never been beaten
   black and blue; the only contestant who can confidently
   enter the lists is the man who has seen his own blood, who
   has felt his teeth rattle beneath his opponent's fist, who has
   been tripped and felt the full force of his adversary's charge,
   who has been downed in body but not in spirit, one who, as
   often as he falls, rises again with greater defiance than ever.

3. So, then, to keep up my figure, Fortune has often in the past
   got the upper hand of you, and yet you have not surrendered,

but have leaped up and stood your ground still more eagerly. For manliness gains much strength by being challenged; nevertheless, if you approve, allow me to offer some additional safeguards by which you may fortify yourself.

4. There are more things, Lucilius, likely to frighten us than there are to crush us; we suffer more often in imagination than in reality. I am not speaking with you in the Stoic strain but in my milder style. For it is our Stoic fashion to speak of all those things, which provoke cries and groans, as unimportant and beneath notice; but you and I must drop such great-sounding words, although, Heaven knows, they are true enough. What I advise you to do is, not to be unhappy before the crisis comes; since it may be that the dangers before which you paled as if they were threatening you, will never come upon you; they certainly have not yet come.

5. Accordingly, some things torment us more than they ought; some torment us before they ought; and some torment us when they ought not to torment us at all. We are in the habit of exaggerating, or imagining, or anticipating, sorrow.

The first of these three faults may be postponed for the present, because the subject is under discussion and the case is still in court, so to speak. That which I should call trifling, you will maintain to be most serious; for of course I know that some men laugh while being flogged, and that others wince at a box on the ear. We shall consider later whether these evils derive their power from their own strength, or from our own weakness.

6. Do me the favour, when men surround you and try to talk you into believing that you are unhappy, to consider not what you hear but what you yourself feel, and to take counsel with your feelings and question yourself independently, because you know your own affairs better than anyone else does. Ask: "Is there any reason why these persons should

condole with me? Why should they be worried or even fear some infection from me, as if troubles could be transmitted? Is there any evil involved, or is it a matter merely of ill report, rather than an evil?" Put the question voluntarily to yourself: "Am I tormented without sufficient reason, am I morose, and do I convert what is not an evil into what is an evil?"

7. You may retort with the question: "How am I to know whether my sufferings are real or imaginary?" Here is the rule for such matters: We are tormented either by things present, or by things to come, or by both. As to things present, the decision is easy. Suppose that your person enjoys freedom and health, and that you do not suffer from any external injury. As to what may happen to it in the future, we shall see later on. To-day there is nothing wrong with it.

8. "But," you say, "something will happen to it." First of all, consider whether your proofs of future trouble are sure. For it is more often the case that we are troubled by our apprehensions, and that we are mocked by that mocker, rumour, which is wont to settle wars, but much more often settles individuals. Yes, my dear Lucilius; we agree too quickly with what people say. We do not put to the test those things which cause our fear; we do not examine into them; we blench and retreat just like soldiers who are forced to abandon their camp because of a dust-cloud raised by stampeding cattle, or are thrown into a panic by the spreading of some unauthenticated rumour.

9. And somehow or other it is the idle report that disturbs us most. For truth has its own definite boundaries, but that which arises from uncertainty is delivered over to guesswork and the irresponsible license of a frightened mind. That is why no fear is so ruinous and so uncontrollable as panic fear. For other fears are groundless, but this fear is witless.

10. Let us, then, look carefully into the matter. It is likely that some troubles will befall us; but it is not a present fact. How often has the unexpected happened! How often has the expected never come to pass! And even though it is ordained to be, what does it avail to run out to meet your suffering? You will suffer soon enough, when it arrives; so look forward meanwhile to better things.

11. What shall you gain by doing this? Time. There will be many happenings meanwhile which will serve to postpone, or end, or pass on to another person, the trials which are near or even in your very presence. A fire has opened the way to flight. Men have been let down softly by a catastrophe. Sometimes the sword has been checked even at the victim's throat. Men have survived their own executioners. Even bad fortune is fickle. Perhaps it will come, perhaps not; in the meantime it is not. So look forward to better things.

12. The mind at times fashions for itself false shapes of evil when there are no signs that point to any evil; it twists into the worst construction some word of doubtful meaning; or it fancies some personal grudge to be more serious than it really is, considering not how angry the enemy is, but to what lengths he may go if he is angry. But life is not worth living, and there is no limit to our sorrows, if we indulge our fears to the greatest possible extent; in this matter, let prudence help you, and contemn with a resolute spirit even when it is in plain sight. If you cannot do this, counter one weakness with another, and temper your fear with hope. There is nothing so certain among these objects of fear that it is not more certain still that things we dread sink into nothing and that things we hope for mock us.

13. Accordingly, weigh carefully your hopes as well as your fears, and whenever all the elements are in doubt, decide in your

own favour; believe what you prefer. And if fear wins a majority of the votes, incline in the other direction anyhow, and cease to harass your soul, reflecting continually that most mortals, even when no troubles are actually at hand or are certainly to be expected in the future, become excited and disquieted. No one calls a halt on himself, when he begins to be urged ahead; nor does he regulate his alarm according to the truth. No one says: "The author of the story is a fool, and he who has believed it is a fool, as well as he who fabricated it." We let ourselves drift with every breeze; we are frightened at uncertainties, just as if they were certain. We observe no moderation. The slightest thing turns the scales and throws us forthwith into a panic.

14. But I am ashamed either to admonish you sternly or to try to beguile you with such mild remedies. Let another say: "Perhaps the worst will not happen." You yourself must say: "Well, what if it does happen? Let us see who wins! Perhaps it happens for my best interests; it may be that such a death will shed credit upon my life." Socrates was ennobled by the hemlock draught. Wrench from Cato's hand his sword, the vindicator of liberty, and you deprive him of the greatest share of his glory.

15. I am exhorting you far too long, since you need reminding rather than exhortation. The path on which I am leading you is not different from that on which your nature leads you; you were born to such conduct as I describe. Hence there is all the more reason why you should increase and beautify the good that is in you.

16. But now, to close my letter, I have only to stamp the usual seal upon it, in other words, to commit thereto some noble message to be delivered to you: "The fool, with all his other faults, has this also,—he is always getting ready to live." Reflect, my esteemed Lucilius, what this saying means, and you will see

how revolting is the fickleness of men who lay down every day new foundations of life, and begin to build up fresh hopes even at the brink of the grave.

17. Look within your own mind for individual instances; you will think of old men who are preparing themselves at that very hour for a political career, or for travel, or for business. And what is baser than getting ready to live when you are already old? I should not name the author of this motto, except that it is somewhat unknown to fame and is not one of those popular sayings of Epicurus which I have allowed myself to praise and to appropriate. Farewell.

ON THE REASONS FOR WITHDRAWING FROM THE WORLD

1. I confess that we all have an inborn affection for our body; I confess that we are entrusted with its guardianship. I do not maintain that the body is not to be indulged at all; but I maintain that we must not be slaves to it. He will have many masters who makes his body his master, who is over-fearful in its behalf, who judges everything according to the body.

2. We should conduct ourselves not as if we ought to live for the body, but as if we could not live without it. Our too-great love for it makes us restless with fears, burdens us with cares, and exposes us to insults. Virtue is held too cheap by the man who counts his body too dear. We should cherish the body with the greatest care; but we should also be prepared, when reason, self-respect, and duty demand the sacrifice, to deliver it even to the flames.

3. Let us, however, in so far as we can, avoid discomforts as well as dangers, and withdraw to safe ground, by thinking continually how we may repel all objects of fear. If I am not mistaken, there are three main classes of these: we fear want, we fear sickness, and we fear the troubles which result from the violence of the stronger.

4. And of all these, that which shakes us most is the dread which hangs over us from our neighbour's ascendancy; for it is accompanied by great outcry and uproar. But the natural evils which I have mentioned,—want and sickness,—steal upon us silently with no shock of terror to the eye or to the ear. The other kind of evil comes, so to speak, in the form of a huge parade. Surrounding it is a retinue of swords and fire and chains and a mob of beasts to be let loose upon the disembowelled entrails of men.

5. Picture to yourself under this head the prison, the cross, the rack, the hook, and the stake which they drive straight through a man until it protrudes from his throat. Think of human limbs torn apart by chariots driven in opposite directions, of the terrible shirt smeared and interwoven with inflammable materials, and of all the other contrivances devised by cruelty, in addition to those which I have mentioned!

6. It is not surprising, then, if our greatest terror is of such a fate; for it comes in many shapes and its paraphernalia are terrifying. For just as the torturer accomplishes more in proportion to the number of instruments which he displays,—indeed, the spectacle overcomes those who would have patiently withstood the suffering,—similarly, of all the agencies which coerce and master our minds, the most effective are those which can make a display. Those other troubles are of course not less serious; I mean hunger, thirst, ulcers of the stomach, and fever that parches our very bowels. They are, however, secret; they have no bluster and no heralding; but these, like huge arrays of war, prevail by virtue of their display and their equipment.

7. Let us, therefore, see to it that we abstain from giving offence. It is sometimes the people that we ought to fear; or sometimes a body of influential oligarchs in the Senate, if the method of governing the State is such that most of the

business is done by that body; and sometimes individuals equipped with power by the people and against the people. It is burdensome to keep the friendship of all such persons; it is enough not to make enemies of them. So the wise man will never provoke the anger of those in power; nay, he will even turn his course, precisely as he would turn from a storm if he were steering a ship.

8. When you travelled to Sicily, you crossed the Straits. The reckless pilot scorned the blustering South Wind,—the wind which roughens the Sicilian Sea and forces it into choppy currents; he sought not the shore on the left, but the strand hard by the place where Charybdis throws the seas into confusion. Your more careful pilot, however, questions those who know the locality as to the tides and the meaning of the clouds; he holds his course far from that region notorious for its swirling waters. Our wise man does the same; he shuns a strong man who may be injurious to him, making a point of not seeming to avoid him, because an important part of one's safety lies in not seeking safety openly; for what one avoids, one condemns.

9. We should therefore look about us, and see how we may protect ourselves from the mob. And first of all, we should have no cravings like theirs; for rivalry results in strife. Again, let us possess nothing that can be snatched from us to the great profit of a plotting foe. Let there be as little booty as possible on your person. No one sets out to shed the blood of his fellow men for the sake of bloodshed,—at any rate very few. More murderers speculate on their profits than give vent to hatred. If you are empty-handed, the highwayman passes you by; even along an infested road, the poor may travel in peace.

10. Next, we must follow the old adage and avoid three things with special care: hatred, jealousy, and scorn. And wisdom alone can show you how this may be done. It is hard to observe a mean; we must be chary of letting the fear of jealousy lead

us into becoming objects of scorn, lest, when we choose not to stamp others down, we let them think that they can stamp us down. The power to inspire fear has caused many men to be in fear. Let us withdraw ourselves in every way; for it is as harmful to be scorned as to be admired.

11. One must therefore take refuge in philosophy; this pursuit, not only in the eyes of good men, but also in the eyes of those who are even moderately bad, is a sort of protecting emblem. For speechmaking at the bar, or any other pursuit that claims the people's attention, wins enemies for a man; but philosophy is peaceful and minds her own business. Men cannot scorn her; she is honoured by every profession, even the vilest among them. Evil can never grow so strong, and nobility of character can never be so plotted against, that the name of philosophy shall cease to be worshipful and sacred.

   Philosophy itself, however, should be practised with calmness and moderation.

12. "Very well, then," you retort, "do you regard the philosophy of Marcus Cato as moderate? Cato's voice strove to check a civil war. Cato parted the swords of maddened chieftains. When some fell foul of Pompey and others fell foul of Caesar, Cato defied both parties at once!"

13. Nevertheless, one may well question whether, in those days, a wise man ought to have taken any part in public affairs, and ask: "What do you mean, Marcus Cato? It is not now a question of freedom; long since has freedom gone to rack and ruin. The question is, whether it is Caesar or Pompey who controls the State. Why, Cato, should you take sides in that dispute? It is no business of yours; a tyrant is being selected. What does it concern you who conquers? The better man may win; but the winner is bound to be the worse man." I have referred to Cato's final rôle. But even in previous years the wise man was not permitted to intervene in such plundering

of the state; for what could Cato do but raise his voice and utter unavailing words? At one time he was "hustled" by the mob and spat upon and forcibly removed from the Forum and marked for exile; at another, he was taken straight to prison from the senate chamber.

14. However, we shall consider later whether the wise man ought to give his attention to politics; meanwhile, I beg you to consider those Stoics who, shut out from public life, have withdrawn into privacy for the purpose of improving men's existence and framing laws for the human race without incurring the displeasure of those in power. The wise man will not upset the customs of the people, nor will he invite the attention of the populace by any novel ways of living.

15. "What, then? Can one who follows out this plan be safe in any case?" I cannot guarantee you this any more than I can guarantee good health in the case of a man who observes moderation; although, as a matter of fact, good health results from such moderation. Sometimes a vessel perishes in harbour; but what do you think happens on the open sea? And how much more beset with danger that man would be, who even in his leisure is not secure, if he were busily working at many things! Innocent persons sometimes perish; who would deny that? But the guilty perish more frequently. A soldier's skill is not at fault if he receives the death-blow through his armour.

16. And finally, the wise man regards the reason for all his actions, but not the results. The beginning is in our own power; fortune decides the issue, but I do not allow her to pass sentence upon myself. You may say: "But she can inflict a measure of suffering and of trouble." The highwayman does not pass sentence when he slays.

17. Now you are stretching forth your hand for the daily gift. Golden indeed will be the gift with which I shall load you;

and, inasmuch as we have mentioned gold, let me tell you how its use and enjoyment may bring you greater pleasure. "He who needs riches least, enjoys riches most." "Author's name, please!" you say. Now, to show you how generous I am, it is my intent to praise the dicta of other schools. The phrase belongs to Epicurus, or Metrodorus, or someone of that particular thinking-shop.

18. But what difference does it make who spoke the words? They were uttered for the world. He who craves riches feels fear on their account. No man, however, enjoys a blessing that brings anxiety; he is always trying to add a little more. While he puzzles over increasing his wealth, he forgets how to use it. He collects his accounts, he wears out the pavement in the Forum, he turns over his ledger,—in short, he ceases to be master and becomes a steward. Farewell.

ON PHILOSOPHY,
THE GUIDE OF LIFE

1. It is clear to you, I am sure, Lucilius, that no man can live a happy life, or even a supportable life, without the study of wisdom; you know also that a happy life is reached when our wisdom is brought to completion, but that life is at least endurable even when our wisdom is only begun. This idea, however, clear though it is, must be strengthened and implanted more deeply by daily reflection; it is more important for you to keep the resolutions you have already made than to go on and make noble ones. You must persevere, must develop new strength by continuous study, until that which is only a good inclination becomes a good settled purpose.

2. Hence you no longer need to come to me with much talk and protestations; I know that you have made great progress. I understand the feelings which prompt your words; they are not feigned or specious words. Nevertheless I shall tell you what I think,—that at present I have hopes for you, but not yet perfect trust. And I wish that you would adopt the same attitude towards yourself; there is no reason why you should put confidence in yourself too quickly and readily. Examine yourself; scrutinize and observe yourself in divers ways; but mark, before all else, whether it is in philosophy or merely in life itself that you have made progress.

3. Philosophy is no trick to catch the public; it is not devised for show. It is a matter, not of words, but of facts. It is not pursued in order that the day may yield some amusement before it is spent, or that our leisure may be relieved of a tedium that irks us. It moulds and constructs the soul; it orders our life, guides our conduct, shows us what we should do and what we should leave undone; it sits at the helm and directs our course as we waver amid uncertainties. Without it, no one can live fearlessly or in peace of mind. Countless things that happen every hour call for advice; and such advice is to be sought in philosophy.

4. Perhaps someone will say: "How can philosophy help me, if Fate exists? Of what avail is philosophy, if God rules the universe? Of what avail is it, if Chance governs everything? For not only is it impossible to change things that are determined, but it is also impossible to plan beforehand against what is undetermined; either God has forestalled my plans, and decided what I am to do, or else Fortune gives no free play to my plans."

5. Whether the truth, Lucilius, lies in one or in all of these views, we must be philosophers; whether Fate binds us down by an inexorable law, or whether God as arbiter of the universe has arranged everything, or whether Chance drives and tosses human affairs without method, philosophy ought to be our defence. She will encourage us to obey God cheerfully, but Fortune defiantly; she will teach us to follow God and endure Chance.

6. But it is not my purpose now to be led into a discussion as to what is within our own control,—if foreknowledge is supreme, or if a chain of fated events drags us along in its clutches, or if the sudden and the unexpected play the tyrant over us; I return now to my warning and my exhortation, that you should not allow the impulse of your spirit to weaken and

grow cold. Hold fast to it and establish it firmly, in order that what is now impulse may become a habit of the mind.

7. If I know you well, you have already been trying to find out, from the very beginning of my letter, what little contribution it brings to you. Sift the letter, and you will find it. You need not wonder at any genius of mine; for as yet I am lavish only with other men's property.—But why did I say "other men"? Whatever is well said by anyone is mine.—This also is a saying of Epicurus: "If you live according to nature, you will never be poor; if you live according to opinion, you will never be rich."

8. Nature's wants are slight; the demands of opinion are boundless. Suppose that the property of many millionaires is heaped up in your possession. Assume that fortune carries you far beyond the limits of a private income, decks you with gold, clothes you in purple, and brings you to such a degree of luxury and wealth that you can bury the earth under your marble floors; that you may not only possess, but tread upon, riches. Add statues, paintings, and whatever any art has devised for the satisfaction of luxury; you will only learn from such things to crave still greater.

9. Natural desires are limited; but those which spring from false opinion can have no stopping point. The false has no limits. When you are travelling on a road, there must be an end; but when astray, your wanderings are limitless. Recall your steps, therefore, from idle things, and when you would know whether that which you seek is based upon a natural or upon a misleading desire, consider whether it can stop at any definite point. If you find, after having travelled far, that there is a more distant goal always in view, you may be sure that this condition is contrary to nature. Farewell.

ON PRACTISING WHAT
YOU PREACH

1. If you are in good health and if you think yourself worthy of becoming at last your own master, I am glad. For the credit will be mine, if I can drag you from the floods in which you are being buffeted without hope of emerging. This, however, my dear Lucilius, I ask and beg of you, on your part, that you let wisdom sink into your soul, and test your progress, not by mere speech or writings, but by stoutness of heart and decrease of desire. Prove your words by your deeds.

2. Far different is the purpose of those who are speech-making and trying to win the approbation of a throng of hearers, far different that of those who allure the ears of young men and idlers by many-sided or fluent argumentation; philosophy teaches us to act, not to speak; it exacts of every man that he should live according to his own standards, that his life should not be out of harmony with his words, and that, further, his inner life should be of one hue and not out of harmony with all his activities. This, I say, is the highest duty and the highest proof of wisdom,—that deed and word should be in accord, that a man should be equal to himself under all conditions, and always the same.

    "But," you reply, "who can maintain this standard?" Very few, to be sure; but there are some. It is indeed a hard undertaking, and I do not say that the philosopher can always keep the same pace. But he can always travel the same path.

3. Observe yourself, then, and see whether your dress and your house are inconsistent, whether you treat yourself lavishly and your family meanly, whether you eat frugal dinners and yet build luxurious houses. You should lay hold, once for all, upon a single norm to live by, and should regulate your whole life according to this norm. Some men restrict themselves at home, but strut with swelling port before the public; such discordance is a fault, and it indicates a wavering mind which cannot yet keep its balance.

4. And I can tell you, further, whence arise this unsteadiness and disagreement of action and purpose; it is because no man resolves upon what he wishes, and, even if he has done so, he does not persist in it, but jumps the track; not only does he change, but he returns and slips back to the conduct which he has abandoned and abjured.

5. Therefore, to omit the ancient definitions of wisdom and to include the whole manner of human life, I can be satisfied with the following: "What is wisdom? Always desiring the same things, and always refusing the same things." You may be excused from adding the little proviso,—that what you wish, should be right; since no man can always be satisfied with the same thing, unless it is right.

6. For this reason men do not know what they wish, except at the actual moment of wishing; no man ever decided once and for all to desire or to refuse. Judgment varies from day to day, and changes to the opposite, making many a man pass his life in a kind of game. Press on, therefore, as you have begun; perhaps you will be led to perfection, or to a point which you alone understand is still short of perfection.

7. "But what," you say, "will become of my crowded household without a household income?" If you stop supporting that crowd, it will support itself; or perhaps you will learn by the bounty of poverty what you cannot learn by your own bounty. Poverty will keep for you your true and tried friends; you will be rid of the men who were not seeking you for yourself, but for something which you have. Is it not true, however, that you should love poverty, if only for this single reason,—that it will show you those by whom you are loved? O when will that time come, when no one shall tell lies to compliment you!

8. Accordingly, let your thoughts, your efforts, your desires, help to make you content with your own self and with the goods that spring from yourself; and commit all your other prayers to God's keeping! What happiness could come closer home to you? Bring yourself down to humble conditions, from which you cannot be ejected; and in order that you may do so with greater alacrity, the contribution contained in this letter shall refer to that subject; I shall bestow it upon you forthwith.

9. Although you may look askance, Epicurus will once again be glad to settle my indebtedness: "Believe me, your words will be more imposing if you sleep on a cot and wear rags. For in that case you will not be merely saying them; you will be demonstrating their truth." I, at any rate, listen in a different spirit to the utterances of our friend Demetrius, after I have seen him reclining without even a cloak to cover him, and, more than this, without rugs to lie upon. He is not only a teacher of the truth, but a witness to the truth.

10. "May not a man, however, despise wealth when it lies in his very pocket?" Of course; he also is great-souled, who sees riches heaped up round him and, after wondering long and deeply because they have come into his possession, smiles,

and hears rather than feels that they are his. It means much not to be spoiled by intimacy with riches; and he is truly great who is poor amidst riches.

11. "Yes, but I do not know," you say, "how the man you speak of will endure poverty, if he falls into it suddenly." Nor do I, Epicurus, know whether the poor man you speak of will despise riches, should he suddenly fall into them; accordingly, in the case of both, it is the mind that must be appraised, and we must investigate whether your man is pleased with his poverty, and whether my man is displeased with his riches. Otherwise, the cot-bed and the rags are slight proof of his good intentions, if it has not been made clear that the person concerned endures these trials not from necessity but from preference.

12. It is the mark, however, of a noble spirit not to precipitate oneself into such things on the ground that they are better, but to practise for them on the ground that they are thus easy to endure. And they are easy to endure, Lucilius; when, however, you come to them after long rehearsal, they are even pleasant; for they contain a sense of freedom from care,— and without this nothing is pleasant.

13. I hold it essential, therefore, to do as I have told you in a letter that great men have often done: to reserve a few days in which we may prepare ourselves for real poverty by means of fancied poverty. There is all the more reason for doing this, because we have been steeped in luxury and regard all duties as hard and onerous. Rather let the soul be roused from its sleep and be prodded, and let it be reminded that nature has prescribed very little for us. No man is born rich. Every man, when he first sees light, is commanded to be content with milk and rags. Such is our beginning, and yet kingdoms are all too small for us! Farewell.

ON REFORMATION

1. With regard to these two friends of ours, we must proceed along different lines; the faults of the one are to be corrected, the other's are to be crushed out. I shall take every liberty; for I do not love this one if I am unwilling to hurt his feelings. "What," you say, "do you expect to keep a forty-year-old ward under your tutelage? Consider his age, how hardened it now is, and past handling!

2. Such a man cannot be re-shaped; only young minds are moulded." I do not know whether I shall make progress; but I should prefer to lack success rather than to lack faith. You need not despair of curing sick men even when the disease is chronic, if only you hold out against excess and force them to do and submit to many things against their will. As regards our other friend I am not sufficiently confident, either, except for the fact that he still has sense of shame enough to blush for his sins. This modesty should be fostered; so long as it endures in his soul, there is some room for hope. But as for this veteran of yours, I think we should deal more carefully with him, that he may not become desperate about himself.

3. There is no better time to approach him than now, when he has an interval of rest and seems like one who has corrected

his faults. Others have been cheated by this interval of virtue on his part, but he does not cheat me. I feel sure that these faults will return, as it were, with compound interest, for just now, I am certain, they are in abeyance but not absent. I shall devote some time to the matter, and try to see whether or not something can be done.

4. But do you yourself, as indeed you are doing, show me that you are stout-hearted; lighten your baggage for the march. None of our possessions is essential. Let us return to the law of nature; for then riches are laid up for us. The things which we actually need are free for all, or else cheap; nature craves only bread and water. No one is poor according to this standard; when a man has limited his desires within these bounds, he can challenge the happiness of Jove himself, as Epicurus says. I must insert in this letter one or two more of his sayings:

5. "Do everything as if Epicurus were watching you." There is no real doubt that it is good for one to have appointed a guardian over oneself, and to have someone whom you may look up to, someone whom you may regard as a witness of your thoughts. It is, indeed, nobler by far to live as you would live under the eyes of some good man, always at your side; but nevertheless I am content if you only act, in whatever you do, as you would act if anyone at all were looking on; because solitude prompts us to all kinds of evil.

6. And when you have progressed so far that you have also respect for yourself, you may send away your attendant; but until then, set as a guard over yourself the authority of some man, whether your choice be the great Cato or Scipio, or Laelius,—or any man in whose presence even abandoned wretches would check their bad impulses. Meantime, you are engaged in making of yourself the sort of person in whose company you would not dare to sin. When this aim has

been accomplished and you begin to hold yourself in some esteem, I shall gradually allow you to do what Epicurus, in another passage, suggests: "The time when you should most of all withdraw into yourself is when you are forced to be in a crowd."

7. You ought to make yourself of a different stamp from the multitude. Therefore, while it is not yet safe to withdraw into solitude, seek out certain individuals; for everyone is better off in the company of somebody or other,—no matter who,— than in his own company alone. "The time when you should most of all withdraw into yourself is when you are forced to be in a crowd." Yes, provided that you are a good, tranquil, and self-restrained man; otherwise, you had better withdraw into a crowd in order to get away from your self. Alone, you are too close to a rascal. Farewell.

ON TRAVEL AS A CURE
FOR DISCONTENT

1. Do you suppose that you alone have had this experience? Are you surprised, as if it were a novelty, that after such long travel and so many changes of scene you have not been able to shake off the gloom and heaviness of your mind? You need a change of soul rather than a change of climate. Though you may cross vast spaces of sea, and though, as our Vergil remarks,

    Lands and cities are left astern,

    your faults will follow you whithersoever you travel.

2. Socrates made the same remark to one who complained; he said: "Why do you wonder that globe-trotting does not help you, seeing that you always take yourself with you? The reason which set you wandering is ever at your heels." What pleasure is there in seeing new lands? Or in surveying cities and spots of interest? All your bustle is useless. Do you ask why such flight does not help you? It is because you flee along with yourself. You must lay aside the burdens of the mind; until you do this, no place will satisfy you.

3. Reflect that your present behaviour is like that of the prophetess whom Vergil describes: she is excited and goaded into

fury, and contains within herself much inspiration that is not her own:

> The priestess raves, if haply she may shake
> The great god from her heart.

You wander hither and yon, to rid yourself of the burden that rests upon you, though it becomes more troublesome by reason of your very restlessness, just as in a ship the cargo when stationary makes no trouble, but when it shifts to this side or that, it causes the vessel to heel more quickly in the direction where it has settled. Anything you do tells against you, and you hurt yourself by your very unrest; for you are shaking up a sick man.

4. That trouble once removed, all change of scene will become pleasant; though you may be driven to the uttermost ends of the earth, in whatever corner of a savage land you may find yourself, that place, however forbidding, will be to you a hospitable abode. The person you are matters more than the place to which you go; for that reason we should not make the mind a bondsman to any one place. Live in this belief: "I am not born for any one corner of the universe; this whole world is my country."

5. If you saw this fact clearly, you would not be surprised at getting no benefit from the fresh scenes to which you roam each time through weariness of the old scenes. For the first would have pleased you in each case, had you believed it wholly yours. As it is, however, you are not journeying; you are drifting and being driven, only exchanging one place for another, although that which you seek,—to live well,—is found everywhere.

6. Can there be any spot so full of confusion as the Forum? Yet you can live quietly even there, if necessary. Of course, if one

were allowed to make one's own arrangements, I should flee far from the very sight and neighbourhood of the Forum. For just as pestilential places assail even the strongest constitution, so there are some places which are also unwholesome for a healthy mind which is not yet quite sound, though recovering from its ailment.

7. I disagree with those who strike out into the midst of the billows and, welcoming a stormy existence, wrestle daily in hardihood of soul with life's problems. The wise man will endure all that, but will not choose it; he will prefer to be at peace rather than at war. It helps little to have cast out your own faults if you must quarrel with those of others.

8. Says one: "There were thirty tyrants surrounding Socrates, and yet they could not break his spirit"; but what does it matter how many masters a man has? "Slavery" has no plural; and he who has scorned it is free,—no matter amid how large a mob of overlords he stands.

9. It is time to stop, but not before I have paid duty. "The knowledge of sin is the beginning of salvation." This saying of Epicurus seems to me to be a noble one. For he who does not know that he has sinned does not desire correction; you must discover yourself in the wrong before you can reform yourself.

10. Some boast of their faults. Do you think that the man has any thought of mending his ways who counts over his vices as if they were virtues? Therefore, as far as possible, prove yourself guilty; hunt up charges against yourself; play the part, first of accuser, then of judge, last of intercessor. At times be harsh with yourself. Farewell.

ON THE GOD WITHIN US

1. You are doing an excellent thing, one which will be wholesome for you, if, as you write me, you are persisting in your effort to attain sound understanding; it is foolish to pray for this when you can acquire it from yourself. We do not need to uplift our hands towards heaven, or to beg the keeper of a temple to let us approach his idol's ear, as if in this way our prayers were more likely to be heard. God is near you, he is with you, he is within you.

2. This is what I mean, Lucilius: a holy spirit indwells within us, one who marks our good and bad deeds, and is our guardian. As we treat this spirit, so are we treated by it. Indeed, no man can be good without the help of God. Can one rise superior to fortune unless God helps him to rise? He it is that gives noble and upright counsel. In each good man

    A god doth dwell, but what god know we not.

3. If ever you have come upon a grove that is full of ancient trees which have grown to an unusual height, shutting out a view of the sky by a veil of pleached and intertwining branches, then the loftiness of the forest, the seclusion of the spot, and your marvel at the thick unbroken shade in the midst of the

open spaces, will prove to you the presence of deity. Or if a cave, made by the deep crumbling of the rocks, holds up a mountain on its arch, a place not built with hands but hollowed out into such spaciousness by natural causes, your soul will be deeply moved by a certain intimation of the existence of God. We worship the sources of mighty rivers; we erect altars at places where great streams burst suddenly from hidden sources; we adore springs of hot water as divine, and consecrate certain pools because of their dark waters or their immeasurable depth.

4.   If you see a man who is unterrified in the midst of dangers, untouched by desires, happy in adversity, peaceful amid the storm, who looks down upon men from a higher plane, and views the gods on a footing of equality, will not a feeling of reverence for him steal over you? Will you not say: "This quality is too great and too lofty to be regarded as resembling this petty body in which it dwells? A divine power has descended upon that man."

5.   When a soul rises superior to other souls, when it is under control, when it passes through every experience as if it were of small account, when it smiles at our fears and at our prayers, it is stirred by a force from heaven. A thing like this cannot stand upright unless it be propped by the divine. Therefore, a greater part of it abides in that place from whence it came down to earth. Just as the rays of the sun do indeed touch the earth, but still abide at the source from which they are sent; even so the great and hallowed soul, which has come down in order that we may have a nearer knowledge of divinity, does indeed associate with us, but still cleaves to its origin; on that source it depends, thither it turns its gaze and strives to go, and it concerns itself with our doings only as a being superior to ourselves.

6.   What, then, is such a soul? One which is resplendent with no external good, but only with its own. For what is more foolish

than to praise in a man the qualities which come from without? And what is more insane than to marvel at characteristics which may at the next instant be passed on to someone else? A golden bit does not make a better horse. The lion with gilded mane, in process of being trained and forced by weariness to endure the decoration, is sent into the arena in quite a different way from the wild lion whose spirit is unbroken; the latter, indeed, bold in his attack, as nature wished him to be, impressive because of his wild appearance,—and it is his glory that none can look upon him without fear,—is favoured in preference to the other lion, that languid and gilded brute.

7. No man ought to glory except in that which is his own. We praise a vine if it makes the shoots teem with increase, if by its weight it bends to the ground the very poles which hold its fruit; would any man prefer to this vine one from which golden grapes and golden leaves hang down? In a vine the virtue peculiarly its own is fertility; in man also we should praise that which is his own. Suppose that he has a retinue of comely slaves and a beautiful house, that his farm is large and large his income; none of these things is in the man himself; they are all on the outside.

8. Praise the quality in him which cannot be given or snatched away, that which is the peculiar property of the man. Do you ask what this is? It is soul, and reason brought to perfection in the soul. For man is a reasoning animal. Therefore, man's highest good is attained, if he has fulfilled the good for which nature designed him at birth.

9. And what is it which this reason demands of him? The easiest thing in the world,—to live in accordance with his own nature. But this is turned into a hard task by the general madness of mankind; we push one another into vice. And how can a man be recalled to salvation, when he has none to restrain him, and all mankind to urge him on? Farewell.

ON THE SHORTNESS OF LIFE

1. A man is indeed lazy and careless, my dear Lucilius, if he is reminded of a friend only by seeing some landscape which stirs the memory; and yet there are times when the old familiar haunts stir up a sense of loss that has been stored away in the soul, not bringing back dead memories, but rousing them from their dormant state, just as the sight of a lost friend's favourite slave, or his cloak, or his house, renews the mourner's grief, even though it has been softened by time.

   Now, lo and behold, Campania, and especially Naples and your beloved Pompeii, struck me, when I viewed them, with a wonderfully fresh sense of longing for you. You stand in full view before my eyes. I am on the point of parting from you. I see you choking down your tears and resisting without success the emotions that well up at the very moment when you try to check them. I seem to have lost you but a moment ago. For what is not "but a moment ago" when one begins to use the memory?

2. It was but a moment ago that I sat, as a lad, in the school of the philosopher Sotion, but a moment ago that I began to plead in the courts, but a moment ago that I lost the desire

to plead, but a moment ago that I lost the ability. Infinitely swift is the flight of time, as those see more clearly who are looking backwards. For when we are intent on the present, we do not notice it, so gentle is the passage of time's headlong flight.

3. Do you ask the reason for this? All past time is in the same place; it all presents the same aspect to us, it lies together. Everything slips into the same abyss. Besides, an event which in its entirety is of brief compass cannot contain long intervals. The time which we spend in living is but a point, nay, even less than a point. But this point of time, infinitesimal as it is, nature has mocked by making it seem outwardly of longer duration; she has taken one portion thereof and made it infancy, another childhood, another youth, another the gradual slope, so to speak, from youth to old age, and old age itself is still another. How many steps for how short a climb!

4. It was but a moment ago that I saw you off on your journey; and yet this "moment ago" makes up a goodly share of our existence, which is so brief, we should reflect, that it will soon come to an end altogether. In other years time did not seem to me to go so swiftly; now, it seems fast beyond belief, perhaps, because I feel that the finish line is moving closer to me, or it may be that I have begun to take heed and reckon up my losses.

5. For this reason I am all the more angry that some men claim the major portion of this time for superfluous things,—time which, no matter how carefully it is guarded, cannot suffice even for necessary things. Cicero declared that if the number of his days were doubled, he should not have time to read the lyric poets. And you may rate the dialecticians in the same class; but they are foolish in a more melancholy way. The lyric

poets are avowedly frivolous; but the dialecticians believe that they are themselves engaged upon serious business.

6. I do not deny that one must cast a glance at dialectic; but it ought to be a mere glance, a sort of greeting from the threshold, merely that one may not be deceived, or judge these pursuits to contain any hidden matters of great worth.

    Why do you torment yourself and lose weight over some problem which it is more clever to have scorned than to solve? When a soldier is undisturbed and travelling at his ease, he can hunt for trifles along his way; but when the enemy is closing in on the rear, and a command is given to quicken the pace, necessity makes him throw away everything which he picked up in moments of peace and leisure.

7. I have no time to investigate disputed inflections of words, or to try my cunning upon them.

    > Behold the gathering clans, the fast-shut gates,
    > And weapons whetted ready for the war.

    I need a stout heart to hear without flinching this din of battle which sounds round about.

8. And all would rightly think me mad if, when greybeards and women were heaping up rocks for the fortifications, when the armour-clad youths inside the gates were awaiting, or even demanding, the order for a sally, when the spears of the foemen were quivering in our gates and the very ground was rocking with mines and subterranean passages,—I say, they would rightly think me mad if I were to sit idle, putting such petty posers as this: "What you have not lost, you have. But you have not lost any horns. Therefore, you have horns," or other tricks constructed after the model of this piece of sheer silliness.

9. And yet I may well seem in your eyes no less mad, if I spend my energies on that sort of thing; for even now I am in a state of siege. And yet, in the former case it would be merely a peril from the outside that threatened me, and a wall that sundered me from the foe; as it is now, death-dealing perils are in my very presence. I have no time for such nonsense; a mighty undertaking is on my hands. What am I to do? Death is on my trail, and life is fleeting away; teach me something with which to face these troubles.

10. Bring it to pass that I shall cease trying to escape from death, and that life may cease to escape from me. Give me courage to meet hardships; make me calm in the face of the unavoidable. Relax the straitened limits of the time which is allotted me. Show me that the good in life does not depend upon life's length, but upon the use we make of it; also, that it is possible, or rather usual, for a man who has lived long to have lived too little. Say to me when I lie down to sleep: "You may not wake again!" And when I have waked: "You may not go to sleep again!" Say to me when I go forth from my house: "You may not return!" And when I return: "You may never go forth again!"

11. You are mistaken if you think that only on an ocean voyage there is a very slight space between life and death. No, the distance between is just as narrow everywhere. It is not everywhere that death shows himself so near at hand; yet everywhere he is as near at hand.

Rid me of these shadowy terrors; then you will more easily deliver to me the instruction for which I have prepared myself. At our birth nature made us teachable, and gave us reason, not perfect, but capable of being perfected.

12. Discuss for me justice, duty, thrift, and that twofold purity, both the purity which abstains from another's person, and

that which takes care of one's own self. If you will only refuse to lead me along bypaths, I shall more easily reach the goal at which I am aiming. For, as the tragic poet says:

> The language of truth is simple.

We should not, therefore, make that language intricate; since there is nothing less fitting for a soul of great endeavour than such crafty cleverness. Farewell.

ON MEETING
DEATH CHEERFULLY

1. Let us cease to desire that which we have been desiring. I, at least, am doing this: in my old age I have ceased to desire what I desired when a boy. To this single end my days and my nights are passed; this is my task, this the object of my thoughts,—to put an end to my chronic ills. I am endeavouring to live every day as if it were a complete life. I do not indeed snatch it up as if it were my last; I do regard it, however, as if it might even be my last.

2. The present letter is written to you with this in mind,—as if death were about to call me away in the very act of writing. I am ready to depart, and I shall enjoy life just because I am not over-anxious as to the future date of my departure.

   Before I became old I tried to live well; now that I am old, I shall try to die well; but dying well means dying gladly. See to it that you never do anything unwillingly.

3. That which is bound to be a necessity if you rebel, is not a necessity if you desire it. This is what I mean: he who takes his orders gladly, escapes the bitterest part of slavery—doing what one does not want to do. The man who does something under orders is not unhappy; he is unhappy who does something against his will. Let us therefore so set our minds in

183

order that we may desire whatever is demanded of us by circumstances, and above all that we may reflect upon our end without sadness.

4. We must make ready for death before we make ready for life. Life is well enough furnished, but we are too greedy with regard to its furnishings; something always seems to us lacking, and will always seem lacking. To have lived long enough depends neither upon our years nor upon our days, but upon our minds. I have lived, my dear friend Lucilius, long enough. I have had my fill; I await death. Farewell.

ON DRUNKENNESS

1. You bid me give you an account of each separate day, and of the whole day too; so you must have a good opinion of me if you think that in these days of mine there is nothing to hide. At any rate, it is thus that we should live,—as if we lived in plain sight of all men; and it is thus that we should think,—as if there were someone who could look into our inmost souls; and there is one who can so look. For what avails it that something is hidden from man? Nothing is shut off from the sight of God. He is witness of our souls, and he comes into the very midst of our thoughts—comes into them, I say, as one who may at any time depart.

2. I shall therefore do as you bid, and shall gladly inform you by letter what I am doing, and in what sequence. I shall keep watching myself continually, and—a most useful habit—shall review each day. For this is what makes us wicked: that no one of us looks back over his own life. Our thoughts are devoted only to what we are about to do. And yet our plans for the future always depend on the past.

3. To-day has been unbroken; no one has filched the slightest part of it from me. The whole time has been divided between rest and reading. A brief space has been given over to bodily exercise, and on this ground I can thank old

age—my exercise costs very little effort; as soon as I stir, I am tired. And weariness is the aim and end of exercise, no matter how strong one is.

4. Do you ask who are my pacemakers? One is enough for me,—the slave Pharius, a pleasant fellow, as you know; but I shall exchange him for another. At my time of life I need one who is of still more tender years. Pharius, at any rate, says that he and I are at the same period of life; for we are both losing our teeth. Yet even now I can scarcely follow his pace as he runs, and within a very short time I shall not be able to follow him at all; so you see what profit we get from daily exercise. Very soon does a wide interval open between two persons who travel different ways. My slave is climbing up at the very moment when I am coming down, and you surely know how much quicker the latter is. Nay, I was wrong; for now my life is not coming down; it is falling outright.

5. Do you ask, for all that, how our race resulted to-day? We raced to a tie,—something which rarely happens in a running contest. After tiring myself out in this way (for I cannot call it exercise), I took a cold bath; this, at my house, means just short of hot. I, the former cold-water enthusiast, who used to celebrate the new year by taking a plunge into the canal, who, just as naturally as I would set out to do some reading or writing, or to compose a speech, used to inaugurate the first of the year with a plunge into the Virgo aqueduct, have changed my allegiance, first to the Tiber, and then to my favourite tank, which is warmed only by the sun, at times when I am most robust and when there is not a flaw in my bodily processes. I have very little energy left for bathing.

6. After the bath, some stale bread and breakfast without a table; no need to wash the hands after such a meal. Then comes a very short nap. You know my habit; I avail myself of a scanty bit of sleep,—unharnessing, as it were. For I am

satisfied if I can just stop staying awake. Sometimes I know that I have slept; at other times, I have a mere suspicion.

7. Lo, now the din of the Races sounds about me! My ears are smitten with sudden and general cheering. But this does not upset my thoughts or even break their continuity. I can endure an uproar with complete resignation. The medley of voices blended in one note sounds to me like the dashing of waves, or like the wind that lashes the tree-tops, or like any other sound which conveys no meaning.

8. What is it, then, you ask, to which I have been giving my attention? I will tell you. A thought sticks in my mind, left over from yesterday,—namely, what men of the greatest sagacity have meant when they have offered the most trifling and intricate proofs for problems of the greatest importance,—proofs which may be true, but none the less resemble fallacies.

9. Zeno, that greatest of men, the revered founder of our brave and holy school of philosophy, wishes to discourage us from drunkenness. Listen, then, to his arguments proving that the good man will not get drunk: "No one entrusts a secret to a drunken man; but one will entrust a secret to a good man; therefore, the good man will not get drunk." Mark how ridiculous Zeno is made when we set up a similar syllogism in contrast with his. There are many, but one will be enough: "No one entrusts a secret to a man when he is asleep; but one entrusts a secret to a good man; therefore, the good man does not go to sleep."

10. Posidonius pleads the cause of our master Zeno in the only possible way; but it cannot, I hold, be pleaded even in this way. For Posidonius maintains that the word "drunken" is used in two ways,—in the one case of a man who is loaded with wine and has no control over himself; in the other, of a man who is accustomed to get drunk, and is a slave to the habit. Zeno,

he says, meant the latter,—the man who is accustomed to get drunk, not the man who is drunk; and no one would entrust to this person any secret, for it might be blabbed out when the man was in his cups.

11. This is a fallacy. For the first syllogism refers to him who is actually drunk and not to him who is about to get drunk. You will surely admit that there is a great difference between a man who is drunk and a drunkard. He who is actually drunk may be in this state for the first time and may not have the habit, while the drunkard is often free from drunkenness. I therefore interpret the word in its usual meaning, especially since the syllogism is set up by a man who makes a business of the careful use of words, and who weighs his language. Moreover, if this is what Zeno meant, and what he wished it to mean to us, he was trying to avail himself of an equivocal word in order to work in a fallacy; and no man ought to do this when truth is the object of inquiry.

12. But let us admit, indeed, that he meant what Posidonius says; even so, the conclusion is false,—that secrets are not entrusted to an habitual drunkard. Think how many soldiers who are not always sober have been entrusted by a general or a captain or a centurion with messages which might not be divulged! With regard to the notorious plot to murder Gaius Caesar,—I mean the Caesar who conquered Pompey and got control of the state,—Tillius Cimber was trusted with it no less than Gaius Cassius. Now Cassius throughout his life drank water; while Tillius Cimber was a sot as well as a brawler. Cimber himself alluded to this fact, saying: "I carry a master? I cannot carry my liquor!"

13. So let each one call to mind those who, to his knowledge, can be ill trusted with wine, but well trusted with the spoken word; and yet one case occurs to my mind, which I shall relate, lest it fall into oblivion. For life should be provided

with conspicuous illustrations. Let us not always be harking back to the dim past.

14. Lucius Piso, the Director of Public Safety at Rome, was drunk from the very time of his appointment. He used to spend the greater part of the night at banquets, and would sleep until noon. That was the way he spent his morning hours. Nevertheless, he applied himself most diligently to his official duties, which included the guardianship of the city. Even the sainted Augustus trusted him with secret orders when he placed him in command of Thrace. Piso conquered that country. Tiberius, too, trusted him when he took his holiday in Campania, leaving behind him in the city many a critical matter that aroused both suspicion and hatred.

15. I fancy that it was because Piso's drunkenness turned out well for the Emperor that he appointed to the office of city prefect Cossus, a man of authority and balance, but so soaked and steeped in drink that once, at a meeting of the Senate, whither he had come after banqueting, he was overcome by a slumber from which he could not be roused, and had to be carried home. It was to this man that Tiberius sent many orders, written in his own hand,—orders which he believed he ought not to trust even to the officials of his household. Cossus never let a single secret slip out, whether personal or public.

16. So let us abolish all such harangues as this: "No man in the bonds of drunkenness has power over his soul. As the very vats are burst by new wine, and as the dregs at the bottom are raised to the surface by the strength of the fermentation; so, when the wine effervesces, whatever lies hidden below is brought up and made visible. As a man overcome by liquor cannot keep down his food when he has over-indulged in wine, so he cannot keep back a secret either. He pours forth impartially both his own secrets and those of other persons."

17. This, of course, is what commonly happens, but so does this,—that we take counsel on serious subjects with those whom we know to be in the habit of drinking freely. Therefore this proposition, which is laid down in the guise of a defence of Zeno's syllogism, is false,—that secrets are not entrusted to the habitual drunkard.

    How much better it is to arraign drunkenness frankly and to expose its vices! For even the middling good man avoids them, not to mention the perfect sage, who is satisfied with slaking his thirst; the sage, even if now and then he is led on by good cheer which, for a friend's sake, is carried somewhat too far, yet always stops short of drunkenness.

18. We shall investigate later the question whether the mind of the sage is upset by too much wine and commits follies like those of the toper; but meanwhile, if you wish to prove that a good man ought not to get drunk, why work it out by logic? Show how base it is to pour down more liquor than one can carry, and not to know the capacity of one's own stomach; show how often the drunkard does things which make him blush when he is sober; state that drunkenness is nothing but a condition of insanity purposely assumed. Prolong the drunkard's condition to several days; will you have any doubt about his madness? Even as it is, the madness is no less; it merely lasts a shorter time.

19. Think of Alexander of Macedon, who stabbed Clitus, his dearest and most loyal friend, at a banquet; after Alexander understood what he had done, he wished to die, and assuredly he ought to have died.

    Drunkenness kindles and discloses every kind of vice, and removes the sense of shame that veils our evil undertakings. For more men abstain from forbidden actions because they are ashamed of sinning than because their inclinations are good.

20. When the strength of wine has become too great and has gained control over the mind, every lurking evil comes forth from its hiding-place. Drunkenness does not create vice, it merely brings it into view; at such times the lustful man does not wait even for the privacy of a bedroom, but without postponement gives free play to the demands of his passions; at such times the unchaste man proclaims and publishes his malady; at such times your cross-grained fellow does not restrain his tongue or his hand. The haughty man increases his arrogance, the ruthless man his cruelty, the slanderer his spitefulness. Every vice is given free play and comes to the front.

21. Besides, we forget who we are, we utter words that are halting and poorly enunciated, the glance is unsteady, the step falters, the head is dizzy, the very ceiling moves about as if a cyclone were whirling the whole house, and the stomach suffers torture when the wine generates gas and causes our very bowels to swell. However, at the time, these troubles can be endured, so long as the man retains his natural strength; but what can he do when sleep impairs his powers, and when that which was drunkenness becomes indigestion?

22. Think of the calamities caused by drunkenness in a nation! This evil has betrayed to their enemies the most spirited and warlike races; this evil has made breaches in walls defended by the stubborn warfare of many years; this evil has forced under alien sway peoples who were utterly unyielding and defiant of the yoke; this evil has conquered by the wine cup those who in the field were invincible.

23. Alexander, whom I have just mentioned, passed through his many marches, his many battles, his many winter campaigns (through which he worked his way by overcoming disadvantages of time or place), the many rivers which flowed from unknown sources, and the many seas, all in safety; it was

intemperance in drinking that laid him low, and the famous death-dealing bowl of Hercules.

24. What glory is there in carrying much liquor? When you have won the prize, and the other banqueters, sprawling asleep or vomiting, have declined your challenge to still other toasts; when you are the last survivor of the revels; when you have vanquished everyone by your magnificent show of prowess and there is no man who has proved himself of so great capacity as you,—you are vanquished by the cask.

25. Mark Antony was a great man, a man of distinguished ability; but what ruined him and drove him into foreign habits and un-Roman vices, if it was not drunkenness and—no less potent than wine—love of Cleopatra? This it was that made him an enemy of the state; this it was that rendered him no match for his enemies; this it was that made him cruel, when as he sat at table the heads of the leaders of the state were brought in; when amid the most elaborate feasts and royal luxury he would identify the faces and hands of men whom he had proscribed; when, though heavy with wine, he yet thirsted for blood. It was intolerable that he was getting drunk while he did such things; how much more intolerable that he did these things while actually drunk!

26. Cruelty usually follows wine-bibbing; for a man's soundness of mind is corrupted and made savage. Just as a lingering illness makes men querulous and irritable and drives them wild at the least crossing of their desires, so continued bouts of drunkenness bestialize the soul. For when people are often beside themselves, the habit of madness lasts on, and the vices which liquor generated retain their power even when the liquor is gone.

27. Therefore you should state why the wise man ought not to get drunk. Explain by facts, and not by mere words, the

hideousness of the thing, and its haunting evils. Do that which is easiest of all—namely, demonstrate that what men call pleasures are punishments as soon as they have exceeded due bounds. For if you try to prove that the wise man can souse himself with much wine and yet keep his course straight, even though he be in his cups, you may go on to infer by syllogisms that he will not die if he swallows poison, that he will not sleep if he takes a sleeping-potion, that he will not vomit and reject the matter which clogs his stomach when you give him hellebore. But, when a man's feet totter and his tongue is unsteady, what reason have you for believing that he is half sober and half drunk? Farewell.

ON THE QUALITY, AS CONTRASTED WITH THE LENGTH, OF LIFE

1. While reading the letter in which you were lamenting the death of the philosopher Metronax as if he might have, and indeed ought to have, lived longer, I missed the spirit of fairness which abounds in all your discussions concerning men and things, but is lacking when you approach one single subject,—as is indeed the case with us all. In other words, I have noticed many who deal fairly with their fellow men, but none who deals fairly with the gods. We rail every day at Fate, saying "Why has A. been carried off in the very middle of his career? Why is not B. carried off instead? Why should he prolong his old age, which is a burden to himself as well as to others?"

2. But tell me, pray, do you consider it fairer that you should obey Nature, or that Nature should obey you? And what difference does it make how soon you depart from a place which you must depart from sooner or later? We should strive, not to live long, but to live rightly; for to achieve long life you have need of Fate only, but for right living you need the soul. A life is really long if it is a full life; but fullness is not attained until the soul has rendered to itself its proper Good, that is, until it has assumed control over itself.

3. What benefit does this older man derive from the eighty years he has spent in idleness? A person like him has not lived; he has merely tarried a while in life. Nor has he died late in life; he has simply been a long time dying. He has lived eighty years, has he? That depends upon the date from which you reckon his death! Your other friend, however, departed in the bloom of his manhood.

4. But he had fulfilled all the duties of a good citizen, a good friend, a good son; in no respect had he fallen short. His age may have been incomplete, but his life was complete. The other man has lived eighty years, has he? Nay, he has existed eighty years, unless perchance you mean by "he has lived" what we mean when we say that a tree "lives."

Pray, let us see to it, my dear Lucilius, that our lives, like jewels of great price, be noteworthy not because of their width but because of their weight. Let us measure them by their performance, not by their duration. Would you know wherein lies the difference between this hardy man who, despising Fortune, has served through every campaign of life and has attained to life's Supreme Good, and that other person over whose head many years have passed? The former exists even after his death; the latter has died even before he was dead.

5. We should therefore praise, and number in the company of the blessed, that man who has invested well the portion of time, however little, that has been allotted to him; for such a one has seen the true light. He has not been one of the common herd. He has not only lived, but flourished. Sometimes he enjoyed fair skies; sometimes, as often happens, it was only through the clouds that there flashed to him the radiance of the mighty star. Why do you ask: "How long did he live?" He still lives! At one bound he has passed over into posterity and has consigned himself to the guardianship of memory.

6. And yet I would not on that account decline for myself a few additional years; although, if my life's space be shortened, I shall not say that I have lacked aught that is essential to a happy life. For I have not planned to live up to the very last day that my greedy hopes had promised me; nay, I have looked upon every day as if it were my last. Why ask the date of my birth, or whether I am still enrolled on the register of the younger men? What I have is my own.

7. Just as one of small stature can be a perfect man, so a life of small compass can be a perfect life. Age ranks among the external things. How long I am to exist is not mine to decide, but how long I shall go on existing in my present way is in my own control. This is the only thing you have the right to require of me,—that I shall cease to measure out an inglorious age as it were in darkness, and devote myself to living instead of being carried along past life.

8. And what, you ask, is the fullest span of life? It is living until you possess wisdom. He who has attained wisdom has reached, not the furthermost, but the most important, goal. Such a one may indeed exult boldly and give thanks to the gods—aye, and to himself also—and he may count himself Nature's creditor for having lived. He will indeed have the right to do so, for he has paid her back a better life than he has received. He has set up the pattern of a good man, showing the quality and the greatness of a good man. Had another year been added, it would merely have been like the past.

9. And yet how long are we to keep living? We have had the joy of learning the truth about the universe. We know from what beginnings Nature arises; how she orders the course of the heavens; by what successive changes she summons back the year; how she has brought to an end all things that ever have been, and has established herself as the only end of her own

being. We know that the stars move by their own motion, and that nothing except the earth stands still, while all the other bodies run on with uninterrupted swiftness. We know how the moon outstrips the sun; why it is that the slower leaves the swifter behind; in what manner she receives her light, or loses it again; what brings on the night, and what brings back the day. To that place you must go where you are to have a closer view of all these things.

10. "And yet," says the wise man, "I do not depart more valiantly because of this hope—because I judge the path lies clear before me to my own gods. I have indeed earned admission to their presence, and in fact have already been in their company; I have sent my soul to them as they had previously sent theirs to me. But suppose that I am utterly annihilated, and that after death nothing mortal remains; I have no less courage, even if, when I depart, my course leads—nowhere."

"But," you say, "he has not lived as many years as he might have lived."

11. There are books which contain very few lines, admirable and useful in spite of their size; and there are also the *Annals of Tanusius*—you know how bulky the book is, and what men say of it. This is the case with the long life of certain persons,—a state which resembles the *Annals of Tanusius*!

12. Do you regard as more fortunate the fighter who is slain on the last day of the games than one who goes to his death in the middle of the festivities? Do you believe that anyone is so foolishly covetous of life that he would rather have his throat cut in the dressing-room than in the amphitheatre? It is by no longer an interval than this that we precede one another. Death visits each and all; the slayer soon follows the slain. It is an insignificant trifle, after all, that people discuss with so much concern. And anyhow, what does it matter for how long a time you avoid that which you cannot escape? Farewell.

ON THE FICKLENESS
OF FORTUNE

1. You need never believe that anyone who depends upon happiness is happy! It is a fragile support—this delight in adventitious things; the joy which entered from without will some day depart. But that joy which springs wholly from oneself is leal and sound; it increases and attends us to the last; while all other things which provoke the admiration of the crowd are but temporary Goods. You may reply: "What do you mean? Cannot such things serve both for utility and for delight?" Of course. But only if they depend on us, and not we on them.

2. All things that Fortune looks upon become productive and pleasant, only if he who possesses them is in possession also of himself, and is not in the power of that which belongs to him. For men make a mistake, my dear Lucilius, if they hold that anything good, or evil either, is bestowed upon us by Fortune; it is simply the raw material of Goods and Ills that she gives to us—the sources of things which, in our keeping, will develop into good or ill. For the soul is more powerful than any sort of Fortune; by its own agency it guides its affairs in either direction, and of its own power it can produce a happy life, or a wretched one.

3. A bad man makes everything bad—even things which had come with the appearance of what is best; but the upright and honest man corrects the wrongs of Fortune, and softens hardship and bitterness because he knows how to endure them; he likewise accepts prosperity with appreciation and moderation, and stands up against trouble with steadiness and courage. Though a man be prudent, though he conduct all his interests with well-balanced judgment, though he attempt nothing beyond his strength, he will not attain the Good which is unalloyed and beyond the reach of threats, unless he is sure in dealing with that which is unsure.

4. For whether you prefer to observe other men (and it is easier to make up one's mind when judging the affairs of others), or whether you observe yourself, with all prejudice laid aside, you will perceive and acknowledge that there is no utility in all these desirable and beloved things, unless you equip yourself in opposition to the fickleness of chance and its consequences, and unless you repeat to yourself often and uncomplainingly, at every mishap, the words: "Heaven decreed it otherwise!"

5. Nay rather, to adopt a phrase which is braver and nearer the truth—one on which you may more safely prop your spirit— say to yourself, whenever things turn out contrary to your expectation: "Heaven decreed *better*!"

    If you are thus poised, nothing will affect you and a man will be thus poised if he reflects on the possible ups and downs in human affairs before he feels their force, and if he comes to regard children, or wife, or property, with the idea that he will not necessarily possess them always and that he will not be any more wretched just because he ceases to possess them.

6. It is tragic for the soul to be apprehensive of the future and wretched in anticipation of wretchedness, consumed with

an anxious desire that the objects which give pleasure may remain in its possession to the very end. For such a soul will never be at rest; in waiting for the future it will lose the present blessings which it might enjoy. And there is no difference between grief for something lost and the fear of losing it.

7. But I do not for this reason advise you to be indifferent. Rather do you turn aside from you whatever may cause fear. Be sure to foresee whatever can be foreseen by planning. Observe and avoid, long before it happens, anything that is likely to do you harm. To effect this your best assistance will be a spirit of confidence and a mind strongly resolved to endure all things. He who can bear Fortune, can also beware of Fortune. At any rate, there is no dashing of billows when the sea is calm. And there is nothing more wretched or foolish than premature fear. What madness it is to anticipate one's troubles!

8. In fine, to express my thoughts in brief compass and portray to you those busybodies and self-tormentors—they are as uncontrolled in the midst of their troubles as they are before them. He suffers more than is necessary, who suffers before it is necessary; such men do not weigh the amount of their suffering, by reason of the same failing which prevents them from being ready for it; and with the same lack of restraint they fondly imagine that their luck will last forever, and fondly imagine that their gains are bound to increase as well as merely continue. They forget this springboard on which mortal things are tossed, and they guarantee for themselves exclusively a steady continuance of the gifts of chance.

9. For this very reason I regard as excellent the saying of Metrodorus, in a letter of consolation to his sister on the loss of her son, a lad of great promise: "All the Good of mortals is mortal." He is referring to those Goods towards which men rush in shoals. For the real Good does not perish; it is certain

and lasting and it consists of wisdom and virtue; it is the only immortal thing that falls to mortal lot.

10. But men are so wayward, and so forgetful of their goal and of the point toward which every day jostles them, that they are surprised at losing anything, although someday they are bound to lose everything. Anything of which you are entitled the owner is in your possession but is not your own; for there is no strength in that which is weak, nor anything lasting and invincible in that which is frail. We must lose our lives as surely as we lose our property, and this, if we understand the truth, is itself a consolation. Lose it with equanimity; for you must lose your life also.

11. What resource do we find, then, in the face of these losses? Simply this—to keep in memory the things we have lost, and not to suffer the enjoyment which we have derived from them to pass away along with them. To have may be taken from us, to have had, never. A man is thankless in the highest degree if, after losing something, he feels no obligation for having received it. Chance robs us of the thing, but leaves us its use and its enjoyment—and we have lost this if we are so unfair as to regret.

12. Just say to yourself: "Of all these experiences that seem so frightful, none is insuperable. Separate trials have been overcome by many: fire by Mucius, crucifixion by Regulus, poison by Socrates, exile by Rutilius, and a sword-inflicted death by Cato; therefore, let us also overcome something."

13. Again, those objects which attract the crowd under the appearance of beauty and happiness, have been scorned by many men and on many occasions. Fabricius when he was general refused riches, and when he was censor branded them with disapproval. Tubero deemed poverty worthy both of himself and of the deity on the Capitol when, by the use

of earthenware dishes at a public festival, he showed that man should be satisfied with that which the gods could still use. The elder Sextius rejected the honours of office; he was born with an obligation to take part in public affairs, and yet would not accept the broad stripe even when the deified Julius offered it to him. For he understood that what can be given can also be taken away.

Let us also, therefore, carry out some courageous act of our own accord; let us be included among the ideal types of history.

14. Why have we been slack? Why do we lose heart? That which could be done, can be done, if only we purify our souls and follow Nature; for when one strays away from Nature one is compelled to crave, and fear, and be a slave to the things of chance. We may return to the true path; we may be restored to our proper state; let us therefore be so, in order that we may be able to endure pain, in whatever form it attacks our bodies, and say to Fortune: "You have to deal with a *man*; seek someone whom you can conquer!"

15. By these words, and words of a like kind, the malignity of the ulcer is quieted down; and I hope indeed that it can be reduced, and either cured or brought to a stop, and grow old along with the patient himself. I am, however, comfortable in my mind regarding him; what we are now discussing is our own loss—the taking-off of a most excellent old man. For he himself has lived a full life, and anything additional may be craved by him, not for his own sake, but for the sake of those who need his services.

16. In continuing to live, he deals generously. Some other person might have put an end to these sufferings; but our friend considers it no less base to flee from death than to flee towards death. "But," comes the answer, "if circumstances warrant, shall he not take his departure?" Of course, if he can no

longer be of service to anyone, if all his business will be to deal with pain.

17. This, my dear Lucilius, is what we mean by studying philosophy while applying it, by practising it on truth—note what courage a prudent man possesses against death, or against pain, when the one approaches and the other weighs heavily. What ought to be done must be learned from one who does it.

18. Up to now we have dealt with arguments—whether any man can resist pain, or whether the approach of death can cast down even great souls. Why discuss it further? Here is an immediate fact for us to tackle—death does not make our friend braver to face pain, nor pain to face death. Rather does he trust himself in the face of both; he does not suffer with resignation because he hopes for death, nor does he die gladly because he is tired of suffering. Pain he endures, death he awaits. Farewell.

ON FACING THE WORLD
WITH CONFIDENCE

1. I shall now tell you certain things to which you should pay attention in order to live more safely. Do you, however,—such is my judgment,—hearken to my precepts just as if I were counselling you to keep safe your health in your country-place at Ardea.

   Reflect on the things which goad man into destroying man: you will find that they are hope, envy, hatred, fear, and contempt.

2. Now, of all these, contempt is the least harmful, so much so that many have skulked behind it as a sort of cure. When a man despises you, he works you injury, to be sure, but he passes on; and no one persistently or of set purpose does hurt to a person whom he despises. Even in battle, prostrate soldiers are neglected: men fight with those who stand their ground.

3. And you can avoid the envious hopes of the wicked so long as you have nothing which can stir the evil desires of others, and so long as you possess nothing remarkable. For people crave even little things, if these catch the attention or are of rare occurrence.

   You will escape envy if you do not force yourself upon the public view, if you do not boast your possessions, if you understand how to enjoy things privately. Hatred comes either from running foul of others: and this can be avoided by never provoking anyone; or else it is uncalled for: and common sense will keep you safe from it. Yet it has been dangerous to many; some people have been hated without having had an enemy.

4. As to not being feared, a moderate fortune and an easy disposition will guarantee you that; men should know that you are the sort of person who can be offended without danger; and your reconciliation should be easy and sure. Moreover, it is as troublesome to be feared at home as abroad; it is as bad to be feared by a slave as by a gentleman. For every one has strength enough to do you some harm. Besides, he who is feared, fears also; no one has been able to arouse terror and live in peace of mind.

5. Contempt remains to be discussed. He who has made this quality an adjunct of his own personality, who is despised because he wishes to be despised and not because he *must* be despised, has the measure of contempt under his control. Any inconveniences in this respect can be dispelled by honourable occupations and by friendships with men who have influence with an influential person; with these men it will profit you to engage but not to entangle yourself, lest the cure may cost you more than the risk.

6. Nothing, however, will help you so much as keeping still—talking very little with others, and as much as may be with yourself. For there is a sort of charm about conversation, something very subtle and coaxing, which, like intoxication or love, draws secrets from us. No man will keep to himself what he hears. No one will tell another only as much as he has heard. And he who tells tales will tell names, too. Everyone has someone to whom he entrusts exactly what has been entrusted to him. Though he checks his own garrulity, and is

content with one hearer, he will bring about him a nation, if that which was a secret shortly before becomes common talk.

7.   The most important contribution to peace of mind is never to do wrong. Those who lack self-control lead disturbed and tumultuous lives; their crimes are balanced by their fears, and they are never at ease. For they tremble after the deed, and they are embarrassed; their consciences do not allow them to busy themselves with other matters, and continually compel them to give an answer. Whoever expects punishment, receives it, but whoever deserves it, expects it.

8.   Where there is an evil conscience something may bring safety, but nothing can bring ease; for a man imagines that, even if he is not under arrest, he may soon be arrested. His sleep is troubled; when he speaks of another man's crime, he reflects upon his own, which seems to him not sufficiently blotted out, not sufficiently hidden from view. A wrongdoer sometimes has the luck to escape notice but never the assurance thereof. Farewell.

ON SELF-CONTROL

1. The question has often been raised whether it is better to have moderate emotions, or none at all. Philosophers of our school reject the emotions; the Peripatetics keep them in check. I, however, do not understand how any halfway disease can be either wholesome or helpful. Do not fear; I am not robbing you of any privileges which you are unwilling to lose! I shall be kindly and indulgent towards the objects for which you strive—those which you hold to be necessary to our existence, or useful, or pleasant; I shall simply strip away the vice. For after I have issued my prohibition against the desires, I shall still allow you to wish that you may do the same things fearlessly and with greater accuracy of judgment, and to feel even the pleasures more than before; and how can these pleasures help coming more readily to your call, if you are their lord rather than their slave!

2. "But," you object, "it is natural for me to suffer when I am bereaved of a friend; grant some privileges to tears which have the right to flow! It is also natural to be affected by men's opinions and to be cast down when they are unfavourable; so why should you not allow me such an honourable aversion to bad opinion?"

There is no vice which lacks some plea; there is no vice that at the start is not modest and easily entreated; but afterwards the trouble spreads more widely. If you allow it to begin, you cannot make sure of its ceasing.

3. Every emotion at the start is weak. Afterwards, it rouses itself and gains strength by progress; it is more easy to forestall it than to forgo it. Who does not admit that all the emotions flow as it were from a certain natural source? We are endowed by Nature with an interest in our own well-being; but this very interest, when overindulged, becomes a vice. Nature has intermingled pleasure with necessary things—not in order that we should seek pleasure, but in order that the addition of pleasure may make the indispensable means of existence attractive to our eyes. Should it claim rights of its own, it is luxury.

Let us therefore resist these faults when they are demanding entrance, because, as I have said, it is easier to deny them admittance than to make them depart.

4. And if you cry: "One should be allowed a certain amount of grieving, and a certain amount of fear," I reply that the "certain amount" can be too long-drawn-out, and that it will refuse to stop short when you so desire. The wise man can safely control himself without becoming overanxious; he can halt his tears and his pleasures at will; but in our case, because it is not easy to retrace our steps, it is best not to push ahead at all.

5. I think that Panaetius gave a very neat answer to a certain youth who asked him whether the wise man should become a lover: "As to the wise man, we shall see later; but you and I, who are as yet far removed from wisdom, should not trust ourselves to fall into a state that is disordered, uncontrolled, enslaved to another, contemptible to itself. If our love be

not spurned, we are excited by its kindness; if it be scorned, we are kindled by our pride. An easily won love hurts us as much as one which is difficult to win; we are captured by that which is compliant, and we struggle with that which is hard. Therefore, knowing our weakness, let us remain quiet. Let us not expose this unstable spirit to the temptations of drink, or beauty, or flattery, or anything that coaxes and allures."

6. Now that which Panaetius replied to the question about love may be applied, I believe, to all the emotions. In so far as we are able, let us step back from slippery places; even on dry ground it is hard enough to take a sturdy stand.

7. At this point, I know, you will confront me with that common complaint against the Stoics: "Your promises are too great, and your counsels too hard. We are mere manikins, unable to deny ourselves everything. We shall sorrow, but not to any great extent; we shall feel desires, but in moderation; we shall give way to anger, but we shall be appeased."

8. And do you know why we have not the power to attain this Stoic ideal? It is because we refuse to believe in our power. Nay, of a surety, there is something else which plays a part: it is because we are in love with our vices; we uphold them and prefer to make excuses for them rather than shake them off. We mortals have been endowed with sufficient strength by nature, if only we use this strength, if only we concentrate our powers and rouse them all to help us or at least not to hinder us. The reason is unwillingness, the excuse, inability. Farewell.

ON THE TRUE GOOD AS ATTAINED BY REASON

1. Full many an ancient precept could I give,

   > Didst thou not shrink, and feel it shame to learn
   > Such lowly duties.

   But you do not shrink, nor are you deterred by any subtleties of study. For your cultivated mind is not wont to investigate such important subjects in a free-and-easy manner. I approve your method in that you make everything count towards a certain degree of progress, and in that you are disgruntled only when nothing can be accomplished by the greatest degree of subtlety. And I shall take pains to show that this is the case now also. Our question is, whether the Good is grasped by the senses or by the understanding; and the corollary thereto is that it does not exist in dumb animals or little children.

2. Those who rate pleasure as the supreme ideal hold that the Good is a matter of the senses; but we Stoics maintain that it is a matter of the understanding, and we assign it to the mind. If the senses were to pass judgment on what is Good, we should never reject any pleasure; for there is no pleasure that does not attract, no pleasure that does not please.

Conversely, we should undergo no pain voluntarily; for there is no pain that does not clash with the senses.

3.   Besides, those who are too fond of pleasure and those who fear pain to the greatest degree would in that case not deserve reproof. But we condemn men who are slaves to their appetites and their lusts, and we scorn men who, through fear of pain, will dare no manly deed. But what wrong could such men be committing if they looked merely to the senses as arbiters of good and evil? For it is to the senses that you and yours have entrusted the test of things to be sought and things to be avoided!

4.   Reason, however, is surely the governing element in such a matter as this; as reason has made the decision concerning the happy life, and concerning virtue and honour also, so she has made the decision with regard to good and evil. For with them the vilest part is allowed to give sentence about the better, so that the senses—dense as they are, and dull, and even more sluggish in man than in the other animals,—pass judgment on the Good.

5.   Just suppose that one should desire to distinguish tiny objects by the touch rather than by the eyesight! There is no special faculty more subtle and acute than the eye, that would enable us to distinguish between good and evil. You see, therefore, in what ignorance of truth a man spends his days and how abjectly he has overthrown lofty and divine ideals, if he thinks that the sense of touch can pass judgment upon the nature of the Supreme Good and the Supreme Evil!

6.   He says: "Just as every science and every art should possess an element that is palpable and capable of being grasped by the senses (their source of origin and growth), even so the happy life derives its foundation and its beginnings from things that are palpable, and from that which falls within the scope

of the senses. Surely you admit that the happy life takes its beginnings from things palpable to the senses."

7. But we define as "happy" those things that are in accord with Nature. And that which is in accord with Nature is obvious and can be seen at once—just as easily as that which is complete. That which is according to Nature, that which is given us as a gift immediately at our birth, is, I maintain, not a Good, but the beginning of a Good. You, however, assign the Supreme Good, pleasure, to mere babies, so that the child at its birth begins at the point whither the perfected man arrives. You are placing the tree-top where the root ought to be.

8. If anyone should say that the child, hidden in its mother's womb, of unknown sex too, delicate, unformed, and shapeless—if one should say that this child is already in a state of goodness, he would clearly seem to be astray in his ideas. And yet how little difference is there between one who has just lately received the gift of life, and one who is still a hidden burden in the bowels of the mother! They are equally developed, as far as their understanding of good or evil is concerned; and a child is as yet no more capable of comprehending the Good than is a tree or any dumb beast.

   But why is the Good nonexistent in a tree or in a dumb beast? Because there is no reason there, either. For the same cause, then, the Good is nonexistent in a child, for the child also has no reason; the child will reach the Good only when he reaches reason.

9. There are animals without reason, there are animals not yet endowed with reason, and there are animals who possess reason, but only incompletely; in none of these does the Good exist, for it is reason that brings the Good in its company. What, then, is the distinction between the classes which I have mentioned? In that which does not possess reason, the

Good will never exist. In that which is not yet endowed with reason, the Good cannot be existent at the time. And in that which possesses reason but only incompletely, the Good is capable of existing, but does not yet exist.

10. This is what I mean, Lucilius: the Good cannot be discovered in any random person, or at any random age; and it is as far removed from infancy as last is from first, or as that which is complete from that which has just sprung into being. Therefore, it cannot exist in the delicate body, when the little frame has only just begun to knit together. Of course not—no more than in the seed.

11. Granting the truth of this, we understand that there is a certain kind of Good of a tree or in a plant; but this is not true of its first growth, when the plant has just begun to spring forth out of the ground. There is a certain Good of wheat: it is not yet existent, however, in the swelling stalk, nor when the soft ear is pushing itself out of the husk, but only when summer days and its appointed maturity have ripened the wheat. Just as Nature in general does not produce her Good until she is brought to perfection, even so man's Good does not exist in man until both reason and man are perfected.

12. And what is this Good? I shall tell you: it is a free mind, an upright mind, subjecting other things to itself and itself to nothing. So far is infancy from admitting this Good that boyhood has no hope of it, and even young manhood cherishes the hope without justification; even our old age is very fortunate if it has reached this Good after long and concentrated study. If this, then, is the Good, the good is a matter of the understanding.

13. "But," comes the retort, "you admitted that there is a certain Good of trees and of grass; then surely there can be a certain Good of a child also." But the true Good is not found

in trees or in dumb animals: the Good which exists in them is called "good" only by courtesy. "Then what is it?" you say. Simply that which is in accord with the nature of each. The real Good cannot find a place in dumb animals—not by any means; its nature is more blessed and is of a higher class. And where there is no place for reason, the Good does not exist.

14. There are four natures which we should mention here: of the tree, animal, man, and God. The last two, having reasoning power, are of the same nature, distinct only by virtue of the immortality of the one and the mortality of the other. Of one of these, then—to wit, God—it is Nature that perfects the Good; of the other—to wit, man—pains and study do so. All other things are perfect only in their particular nature, and not truly perfect, since they lack reason.

Indeed, to sum up, that alone is perfect which is perfect according to nature as a whole, and nature as a whole is possessed of reason. Other things can be perfect according to their kind.

15. That which cannot contain the happy life cannot contain that which produces the happy life; and the happy life is produced by Goods alone. In dumb animals there is not a trace of the happy life, nor of the means whereby the happy life is produced; in dumb animals the Good does not exist.

16. The dumb animal comprehends the present world about him through his senses alone. He remembers the past only by meeting with something which reminds his senses; a horse, for example, remembers the right road only when he is placed at the starting-point. In his stall, however, he has no memory of the road, no matter how often he may have stepped along it. The third state—the future—does not come within the ken of dumb beasts.

17. How, then, can we regard as perfect the nature of those who have no experience of time in its perfection? For time is three-fold,—past, present, and future. Animals perceive only the time which is of greatest moment to them within the limits of their coming and going—the present. Rarely do they recollect the past—and that only when they are confronted with present reminders.

18. Therefore the Good of a perfect nature cannot exist in an imperfect nature; for if the latter sort of nature should possess the Good, so also would mere vegetation. I do not indeed deny that dumb animals have strong and swift impulses toward actions which seem according to nature, but such impulses are confused and disordered. The Good, however, is never confused or disordered.

19. "What!" you say, "do dumb animals move in disturbed and ill-ordered fashion?" I should say that they moved in disturbed and ill-ordered fashion, if their nature admitted of order; as it is, they move in accordance with their nature. For that is said to be "disturbed" which can also at some other time be "not disturbed"; so, too, that is said to be in a state of trouble which can be in a state of peace. No man is vicious except one who has the capacity of virtue; in the case of dumb animals their motion is such as results from their nature.

20. But, not to weary you, a certain sort of good will be found in a dumb animal, and a certain sort of virtue, and a certain sort of perfection—but neither the Good, nor virtue, nor perfection in the absolute sense. For this is the privilege of reasoning beings alone, who are permitted to know the cause, the degree, and the means. Therefore, good can exist only in that which possesses reason.

21. Do you ask now whither our argument is tending, and of what benefit it will be to your mind? I will tell you: it exercises and sharpens the mind, and ensures, by occupying it honourably, that it will accomplish some sort of good. And even that is beneficial which holds men back when they are hurrying into wickedness. However, I will say this also: I can be of no greater benefit to you than by revealing the Good that is rightly yours, by taking you out of the class of dumb animals, and by placing you on a level with God.

22. Why, pray, do you foster and practise your bodily strength? Nature has granted strength in greater degree to cattle and wild beasts. Why cultivate your beauty? After all your efforts, dumb animals surpass you in comeliness. Why dress your hair with such unending attention? Though you let it down in Parthian fashion, or tie it up in the German style, or, as the Scythians do, let it flow wild—yet you will see a mane of greater thickness tossing upon any horse you choose, and a mane of greater beauty bristling upon the neck of any lion. And even after training yourself for speed, you will be no match for the hare.

23. Are you not willing to abandon all these details—wherein you must acknowledge defeat, striving as you are for something that is not your own—and come back to the Good that is really yours?

    And what is this Good? It is a clear and flawless mind, which rivals that of God, raised far above mortal concerns, and counting nothing of its own to be outside itself. You are a reasoning animal. What Good, then, lies within you? Perfect reason. Are you willing to develop this to its farthest limits—to its greatest degree of increase?

24. Only consider yourself happy when all your joys are born of reason, and when—having marked all the objects which men clutch at, or pray for, or watch over—you find nothing which

you will desire; mind, I do not say *prefer*. Here is a short rule by which to measure yourself, and by the test of which you may feel that you have reached perfection: "You will come to your own when you shall understand that those whom the world calls fortunate are really the most unfortunate of all." Farewell.